Teacher Supervision through Behavioral Objectives

Teacher Supervision through Behavioral Objectives

An Operationally Described System

by

Terrence J. Piper, Ph.D.
Professor and Chairperson,
Department of Special Education,
Temple University, Philadelphia

and

Denise B. Elgart, Ed.D.
Supervisor of Education,
CORA Services, Philadelphia

·P·A·U·L·H·
BROOKES
PUBLISHERS

Baltimore

Paul H. Brookes, Publishers
Post Office Box 10624
Baltimore, Maryland 21204

Copyright 1979 by Paul H. Brookes Publishing Co., Inc.
All rights reserved.

Typeset by The Composing Room of Michigan, Inc. (Grand Rapids)
Manufactured in the United States of America by the Maple Press Company
(York, Pennsylvania)

Library of Congress Cataloging in Publication Data

Piper, Terrence J   1943-
    Teacher supervision through behavioral objectives.

    Bibliography: p.
    Includes index.
    1. School supervision. I. Elgart, Denise B.,
1948–   joint author. II. Title.
LB2822.P53   371.2'013   79-15648
ISBN 0-933716-03-6

Contents

Illustrations

Foreword

By **Norris G. Haring**

The teacher supervisor is the person essential to the monitoring and refinement of the educational process. This person is the most logical one in a school system to be the agent for a change in the methods of classroom instruction. This book lays out in detail a comprehensive plan for supervisors and their administrators to follow which guarantees a more objective, verifiable means of observing, measuring, and commenting upon the interaction behaviors of classroom teachers and their students than has been heretofore available. The need for such a system is paramount when we stop to consider that the supervisor is also the primary intermediary between the administrator, educational researcher (developing new curricula and teaching techniques), and the classroom teacher. Accurate, meaningful supervision, when conducted in a systematic, quantifiable manner, offers the best indicator of whether skills being used are successful and appropriate.

There is a great need for a book like this and it is my hope that it will be widely read and its ideas widely disseminated. Much of the effectiveness and quality of instruction depend upon supervision of classroom teachers and how quickly they get new materials. It is additionally important to note that it is this position of supervisor that is frequently cut back in times of fiscal emergencies such as those facing many public school systems today.

Piper and Elgart give an opening overview of teacher supervision and outline ideal job responsibilities and methods for the profession. They give the reader a helpful run-down on current teacher assessment models in use and offer their own, more specific one in the course of the book. In subsequent chapters, issues such as measurement of teacher rapport, observing individualized instruction (especially important with teachers of handicapped children), and the delicate but imperative matter of providing feedback to the teacher, are covered in depth. All told, the authors explain a system for observing and recording the teaching process which is as adaptable to a multihandicapped preschool class as to an advanced trigonometry section in a senior high school. They provide forms which have been fully field-tested over a period of years. The bonus provided is a teacher assessment which may then be translated into realistic and individualized improvement goals for each teacher. In this way, the teaching supervisor may apply the results of an observation system to the area of preservice and inservice skill building as well as using it as a gauge to measure different classroom teaching methods.

Who are teacher supervisors? They are the management personnel, the "action" intermediaries between central administration offices of a school system and the "front lines" of the classroom. They are teachers who have advanced through the teaching ranks of any given discipline and are the most qualified of all to demonstrate effective practices, use the most advanced instructional technology available, and be responsible for staff training and development.

Teacher Supervision through Behavioral Objectives is of unusual value because it stresses three very important activities. First, through the well-trained supervisor, the teacher may learn how to apply learning and behavioral principles in the classroom. Second, the supervisor is the person who can demonstrate the benefits of systematic instruction in the arrangement and implementation of the instructional program. Third, this book describes and *advances* techniques necessary for the teacher to use through the development and training of supervisors who measure behavioral change as it occurs in the classroom. It is only through the systematic arrangement of the learning environment and the continuous measurement of performance change that education will continue to become more refined and develop its rightful status as an applied science.

Throughout American education today, administrators are making many educational decisions that crucially affect the classroom teacher; *yet very often these decisions are not based on classroom performance data at all*. They emerge out of broader social issues and involve politics, economics, and, in some cases, demographic redistribution of students based on race. Often, such decisions do not really have a good reason for being made. Piper and Elgart establish herein a better basis for administrators to begin to have available performance data upon which to base administrative decisions touching classroom teachers. They make a plea for such decisions to be made on the basis of performance data in order that the validity of the decisions may be checked. Until we are able to do this, to assure that administrators—through supervisors—have the information they need, we may expect to see educational strategies, policies, and decisions continue to swing from left to right. This book establishes firmly such a basis for acquiring that information.

Somehow, we must motivate educators to become highly competent professionals. Professional competence is predicated on the systematic refinement of skills through the process of analyzing the effectiveness of the educational plan, measuring the change effected by the plan, and making changes in the plan according to what is indicated by the measurement. In this way, educators' abilities may be developed much in the same way any other applied scientists' are developed. It seems to me that it follows that any discipline advances toward greater effectiveness as the individuals within that discipline advance their skills.

I think it is necessary for teachers to develop a more intense interest in advancing their professional effectiveness and status since they have such a tremendously important influence in shaping the lives of children. It is important that they take those influential powers seriously. This document shows the way for teachers to do their own classroom research and to develop new ideas about educational programming and curriculum in the most successful arrangement of the learning environment.

Finally, it is really the job of the supervisory force of any school district to provide the motivation for this kind of professional development and to inspire teachers to arrange learning opportunities for their children in the most effective way possible. *Teacher Supervision through Behavioral Objectives* provides an excellent guide for achieving these goals.

Preface

We believe that the process of teacher supervision can be the greatest contributing factor in improving the quality of education. Buildings, buses, materials, counselors, administrators, and other supportive services contribute to an outstanding educational environment for children, but it is the teacher who, by far, contributes the most. Without good teachers, the best and most sophisticated system in the world will be mediocre at best. It is the teacher who is directly responsible for the curriculum and classroom environment that the child experiences.

Similarly, it is the teacher's supervisor who is in the best position to improve teacher performance. Through direct observation in the classroom, the supervisor can provide the most relevant and continuous in-service training to the teacher and can serve as a feedback agent regarding the teacher's performance. When the higher administrative structures provide both the time to supervise and the power to evaluate, the supervisor will also have the authority to maximally promote desirable changes. The text that follows is designed to describe a system, easily modified for local needs, by which the supervisor can most effectively perform his or her role.

In most school systems, the supervisory role is considered to be the first or lowest level in the administrative structure. Except for the local school administrators, such as principals, it is also the supervisory role that provides for direct contact between central administrative offices and teachers. Because of the position that supervisors are in, they are typically assigned tasks more closely related to communication between central administration and local schools at the expense of time for direct supervision. Safeguards need to be engineered to protect the primary role of the supervisor from constant pressures to be filling other administrative or clerical roles. We believe that the best practice, in this regard, is to develop a supervisory procedure that is not only effective and adaptable to a variety of situations but that also has a formally defined beginning and end. When this is the case, the teachers' union or supervisors' superiors can then require some minimal number of formal supervisions per teacher per year. The priority of direct supervision will gradually rise to the top as deadlines approach.

For optimal value, the system also needs to be objective. Large amounts of subjective supervision will not necessarily improve anything and are likely to promote teacher resentment. Personal opinions or ratings are to be avoided. Rather, the supervisor should serve as an objective observer and data collector, and the data must be pertinent to the qualities of good teaching. *This text operationally defines the qualities that good teachers display and then provides the forms and means for measuring those qualities.* Once the data is collected it must be shared with the teacher. Feedback is essential if the teacher is to improve his or her behavior. Once the feedback is understood and minimally subject to the supervisor's personal opinion, both individuals can cooperate in establishing a behavioral objective(s) for the teacher. The teacher in turn can concentrate on the area addressed by the objective and, hopefully, improve before the next observation. When the objective is well formulated, improvement can be accurately measured and recorded over time. A minimum of three or four complete supervisory observations per school year are needed for the system to be meaningful.

The first chapter will introduce the reader to the variety of supervisory techniques available today in education. The chapters that follow are designed to describe the format and procedures in a supervisory technique that is innovatively data-based and simul-

taneously takes into account the concerns of the traditional supervisor. Rating scales are avoided so as to minimize subjective
connotations and personal value judgments.

The technique has been employed with great success and
satisfaction in many country-wide administrative units of special education, in university practicum settings, and in research.
Both supervisors and teachers prefer it to other, more traditional
systems.

Acknowledgments

The authors' gratitude is extended to the Supervisory Staff of the Chester County (Pennsylvania) Intermediate Unit who contributed greatly to the development of the material on quality individualization in Chapter 3. The Supervisors were William Benson, George Golden, Phyllis LaDrew, Doyle Lynn, Robert Maier, Cecil Tate, and Bruce Taylor. Phyllis LaDrew is to be specially acknowledged for her contributions. Robert Hurst, Director of Diagnostic and Consultative Services, and Sara Tollinger, Director of Special Education, gave both direction and support.

Dedication

To Sara Tollinger, for initiating the effort represented here, and to the ones we love.

Chapter 1
Models of Teacher Supervision

ROLE OF SUPERVISOR

Teacher supervision and subsequent evaluation are concerned with the development or training of teachers who function well in a classroom situation. Through various techniques, professionals in the field of education can observe and describe a teacher's behavior in order to judge whether it is appropriate or inappropriate.

Historical Perspective: Evolution of Role

According to the account given by Marks, Stoops, and King-Stoops (1978), the purpose and function of supervision has changed throughout this country's history. During the years between the Colonial Period and the Civil War, the major reason for observing teachers was to ensure that the intellectual, social, and spiritual mores of the community were reflected in the classroom. Committees of laymen, clergy, and school wardens and trustees were appointed to inspect classrooms and courses of study in order to determine the extent to which those values were being upheld. Observation instruments were ambiguous in nature and varied from community to community. The Nineteenth Century was marked by the emergence of the role of the school principal. The principal's supervisory authority was acquired gradually. In many cases, local committees of laymen (also known as school boards) were reluctant to relinquish their power over the schools. However, because of the rapid growth of school systems, school boards found it impossible to provide the same direct supervision and control as they had in the past. At first, the principal's duties included only those that were clerical in nature. Later, the responsibilities included discipline of students, school administration, and teacher supervision. By the late 1930's and 1940's, emphasis was placed on research rather than the mere preservation of values of community members. As a result of the intense interest in measurement hallmarked by the mental testing movement, observational techniques and elaborate rating systems were developed so that researchers could accurately record what was happening in the classroom. Unfortunately, emphasis usually was placed on a teacher's weakness and need for improvement. During the 1940's to the early 1960's, the responsibility for teacher supervision shifted away from the principal and was assumed by such professionals as curriculum coordinators, program directors, consultants, and special supervisors. Supervision became program-centered; emphasis was placed on instructional methods and techniques. In-service training was offered so that teachers could become familiar with new materials and instructional aids that were available. From the early 1960's to the present time, teacher supervision has become even more systematic. The surge of systematic observational techniques is the result of the emergence of managerial or behavioral objectives used in education today.

The purposes, techniques, and even the people doing the supervising have changed throughout the years. With the addition of personnel serving in various capacities in large urban school systems across the nation, the responsibility for observing and evaluating teachers has been placed on supervisors. The position of supervisor has been created in order to relieve other administrators of those responsibilities.

Present-Day Role

Duties   The role of the supervisor has evolved into a complex one. According to Lucio and McNeil (1962), there are six discrete duties which supervisors perform.

1. **Planning:** Supervisors help develop programs and policies. If a supervisor is in charge of a particular program (*e.g.*, severely and profoundly impaired program, reading program, or preschool program), then he/she is responsible for developing or determining the content, techniques, and plans to be used by the teachers.
2. **Administration:** Supervisors are the decision-makers concerning policy changes.
3. **Supervision:** Supervisors are responsible for the improvement of the quality of teaching.
4. **Curriculum Development:** Supervisors may prepare teaching guides which set objectives and methods and materials in teaching a content area.
5. **Demonstration Teaching:** Supervisors may actually teach desired lessons for teachers in order to help them achieve the needed teaching skills.
6. **Research:** Supervisors explore, study, and recommend changes on the basis of data collected during classroom observations.

Problems   As one can see, the role of the supervisor is not only complex but extremely time consuming. It is difficult for a supervisor to function well in all aspects of the job since only a limited amount of time is available. If a supervisor is expected to attend all administrative meetings, write curriculum materials, keep abreast of new developments in the field, and conduct research, then little time is left for the actual supervision of teachers. This aspect of the job is not only the most important but also the one compromised most often.

Since the ultimate goal of supervision is the improvement of the products of instruction (Barr, 1931), the supervisor must find time to observe teacher and pupil behavior in the classroom. It is the supervisor's responsibility to analyze the teaching situation and discuss it with the teacher. The supervisor is to provide emotional support and supply information which will be useful in the classroom.

Ideal Supervisory Responsibilities

Division of Supervisory Responsibility Because of the complexity of roles a supervisor must assume in a school system, there is a need to carefully delineate the job. Ideally, the position should be divided into three different jobs:

1. Administrative supervisor
2. Curriculum supervisor
3. Classroom supervisor

The main function of the *administrative supervisor* would be to attend meetings and make decisions concerning policies. The *curriculum supervisor's* role would be to write, implement, and validate new teaching guides and objectives. The role of the *classroom supervisor* would be to observe teacher behavior, demonstrate teaching skills and materials, provide information, lend emotional support, and evaluate the progress of teachers. The three supervisors would be encouraged to share information and work together cooperatively.

Responsibilities of Classroom Supervisor The job of the classroom supervisor is the heart of the school system. The development and training of good teachers promotes learning. The classroom supervisor, however, must have knowledge of certain skills in order to be effective. The supervisor must be familiar with the principles of learning. Supervisors must be able to:

1. Define objectives clearly (in observable and measurable ways)
2. Set up criteria for correct and incorrect responses
3. Determine appropriate reinforcement
4. Arrange the learning environment in order to elicit correct responses
5. Provide transfer of learning-generalizability
6. Provide opportunity for practice or review

These principles of learning apply not only to pupil learning but to teacher learning as well.

Therefore, the ideal responsibilities of the classroom supervisor are to improve the quality of teaching by:

1. Observing what is happening in the classroom
2. Recording the teacher and pupil behavior
3. Giving the teacher feedback concerning what is observed
4. Providing helpful suggestions for improvement when necessary
5. Demonstrating skills when appropriate
6. Observing the progress or change in classroom behavior

The classroom supervisor serves as a teacher trainer, resource for information, and evaluator.

DEVELOPMENT OF TEACHER OBSERVATION MODELS

Need for Models

In order to improve teacher behavior in the classroom, a supervisor must be able to objectively and systematically study and record that which is happening. Tests, rating scales, questionnaires, interviews, and observation forms have all been used to analyze teacher effectiveness (Barr, 1931). According to Bennie (1972), the most desirable instrument for evaluation is one that describes behavior in both observable and measurable terms. An observation device must also be reliable and valid.

Basic Areas of Evaluation

Most evaluation forms used by school systems encompass three basic areas of evaluation (Bennie, 1972). These include items describing a teacher's:

1. Personal characteristics (health; voice; emotional stability; grooming; etc.)
2. Professional and academic background and proficiency (knowledge of subject matter; professional principles; receptivity to suggestions and criticism)

3. Competency in actual teaching (curriculum programming; lesson planning; classroom management)

Sample Observation Models

Commonwealth of Pennsylvania Rating Sheet   Although the observation forms used throughout the nation's school systems may vary slightly in structure and content, they are generally similar in nature. The Rating Sheet used in the Commonwealth of Pennsylvania (Figure 1, page 7) provides a typical checklist on which teachers are evaluated for continued employment.

Categories within Model   The four major categories on which teachers are evaluated include:

1. Personality
2. Preparation
3. Technique
4. Pupil reaction

These categories are then broken down further. The areas included under *personality* appear to encompass an examination of the teacher's ability to relate and interact with others. *Preparation* deals mainly with the amount of subject knowledge and background which the teacher possesses in order to perform his/ her role in the classroom. *Technique* includes a list of actual teaching skills which may be observed in the classroom. The last category, *pupil reaction,* deals with the manner in which students behave and progress. Upon completing the desired number of observations, the supervisor places a check mark next to the area or skill that the teacher possesses or has exhibited. An overall rating of satisfactory or unsatisfactory is then given.

Evaluation of Model   However, inasmuch as most of the categories on the evaluation form are neither adequately defined nor objective in nature, it is difficult to determine or observe such things as a teacher's emotional stability, civic responsibility, and appreciation and ideals. Through the use of such abstract terms, a supervisor is forced to become opinionated and highly subjective.

Commonwealth of Pennsylvania
DEPARTMENT OF EDUCATION
Box 911, Harrisburg, Pa. 17126

Temporary and Professional Employe's Rating Sheet

Last Name	First Name	Middle Name

District (I.U.)	School	Subject(s)	Grade(s)

Satisfactory				Unsatisfactory			
Service of employe sufficiently acceptable to justify continuation of employment.	Name of Person			Improvement is essential to justify continuance in service.	Name of Person		
	Rating				Rating		
	Position		Date		Position		Date

	I PERSONALITY		II PREPARATION		III TECHNIQUE		IV PUPIL REACTION
	1. Physical Characteristics		1. Professional Attitudes		1. Planning and Organization		1. Enthusiasm
	2. Emotional Stability		2. Technical Knowledge and Skill		2. Individualization		2. Power to Appraise
	3. Social Adjustment		3. Continuity of Prof'l Growth		3. Classroom Generalship		3. Normal Development
	4. Professional Relationships		4. Subject Matter Scholarship		4. Manipulation of Materials		4. Expression
	5. Judgment		5. Language Usage		5. Ability to Compromise		5. Subject Matter Progress
	6. Habits of Conduct		6. Civic Responsibility		6.		6. Habits of Thinking
	7.		7. Dependability		7.		7. Habits of Conduct
	8.		8. Appreciation and Ideals		8.		8. Attitudes
	9.		9.		9.		9.

GENERAL RATING

1. Each school official who rates an employe should use a rating card for each rating given.

2. The responsible school official will first rate the employe in general terms of satisfactory or unsatisfactory. If an employe is to be rated satisfactory, the signature of the person doing the rating must be in the block opposite satisfactory; if unsatisfactory, in the block opposite unsatisfactory.

3. Ratings should have the support of anecdotal records. In the case of UNSATISFACTORY ratings, such records must be maintained in the office of the superintendent of schools and a copy supplied to the employe immediately after it has been completed.

Rating _____ Seniority _____ Total _____

Use "FINAL RATING" when reporting to School Boards or Department of Education. "FINAL RATING" may represent a number of separate ratings during period of employment.

DETAILED APPRAISAL

1. When an unsatisfactory rating is given an employe, the school official must place a check in the block opposite that rating.

2. In this respect it is entirely possible that a gross deficiency in a single quality might be sufficiently serious to warrant a total rating of unsatisfactory even though other items were not marked at all.

3. Whenever an unsatisfactory rating is given, each such recorded rating must be stated and the specific circumstances cited. The record must include specific details of evidence likely to be important, in case the services of a teacher are to be discontinued or dismissed.

Final Rating: SATISFACTORY

I certify that the above-named employe has taught for _____ years _____ months under my supervision from _____ to _____ , and has received from me a final rating of "SATISFACTORY."

_____ Date   _____ I.U. Director or Dist. Superintendent

DEBE-333 (5-72)

Final Rating: UNSATISFACTORY

I certify that the above-named employe has taught for _____ years _____ months under my supervision from _____ to _____ , and has received from me a final rating of "UNSATISFACTORY."

_____ Date   _____ I.U. Director or Dist. Superintendent

Figure 1. Temporary and professional employee's rating sheet, Commonwealth of Pennsylvania Rating Scale [DEBE-333 (5-72)].

Minneapolis Public School Observation Form *Categories within Model* The observation form used by the Minneapolis Public Schools (Figure 2, pages 10-17) evaluates a teacher in three major areas

1. Relationship to pupils, staff, and parents
2. Personal qualities
3. Learning activities

The three major areas are broken down into more specific points of observation. The principal or supervisor rates the teacher by placing a check mark on the continuum indicating the extent to which those specific behaviors are exhibited. Additional comments may also be included on the sheet. The categories of behavior are generally chosen due to their observability and subsequent measurability.

Evaluation of Model Even though the categories in this particular observation form are fairly well defined, they are still subject to observer bias. The observer is still rating rather than collecting data. Therefore, all of the difficulties related to relying solely on the observer's opinion come into play. In order for those areas to be objectively evaluated, they must be more adequately defined so that they may lend themselves to direct and precise measurement.

Evaluation of Teaching Form (Temple University) Evaluation forms may not include all three major areas of concern but may focus on just the actual teaching process. The Evaluation of Teaching Form (Temple University, 1976) is shown in Figure 3 (pages 18-21).

Categories within Model Good teaching includes:

1. Using assessment procedures (formal and informal)
2. Writing and following a sequence of behavioral objectives
3. Using appropriate materials
4. Involving pupils in learning activities
5. Managing social and academic behaviors in the classroom

Evaluation of Model This evaluation form selects specific areas to be observed but is also subjective in nature. For example, it is difficult to objectively observe and measure whether all pupils find the lesson clear and interesting. A means for adequately measuring such areas would have to be developed for the system to be objective.

DEVELOPMENT OF MORE COMPREHENSIVE TEACHER OBSERVATION MODELS

Simon and Boyer (1974)

With the present thrust toward evaluating teachers on the basis of concrete, observable variables rather than abstract qualities has come the development of various comprehensive observation models. Simon and Boyer (1974) report 92 observation instruments and describe the major characteristics of each. Table 1 lists 79 observation systems and rates them according to the following seven distinct categories:

1. Affective
2. Cognitive
3. Psychomotor
4. Activity
5. Content
6. Sociological structure
7. Physical environment

Simon and Boyer describe the seven categories and explain how each observation system is classified. The *affective* category focuses on emotions or feelings involved in communication whereas the *cognitive* category emphasizes the information or ideas which are set forth. At times, it is difficult to discriminate between affect (feelings) and cognition (ideas). The third category, *psychomotor,* deals with observation of body movements—posture, facial expression, gestures, etc. *Activity,* the fourth category, also deals with nonverbal behavior. However, with this type of an observation category, the activity in which the person is engaged is of prime importance. Examples may include looking at a film strip, hitting a classmate, or reading a book. *Content* focuses on what is being talked about. Statements of this nature would include those concerning working procedures, assignments, and administrative

MINNEAPOLIS PUBLIC SCHOOLS
Department of Personnel

STATEMENT CONCERNING WORK OF TEACHER AND RECOMMENDATION FOR RE-EMPLOYMENT

Name _____   Grade or Subject _____

School _____   Year _____   Date of Employment _____

The purpose of this evaluation is to determine eligibility for re-employment. A minimum of three visits and conferences is suggested before filing this form. Every item need not be checked. It is possible that other items may be inserted.

This form is completed in triplicate. A copy is given to the teacher, a copy is filed in the school office, and a copy is submitted to the Personnel Department each of the probationary years. For teachers whose anniversary date is the opening of school in the fall, it must be filed by February 15. For those whose starting date does not coincide with fall opening, it must be filed at least sixty (60) days before the anniversary of effective date of appointment.

I. RELATIONSHIP TO PUPILS, STAFF, AND PARENTS

Pupils

| Does not accept certain individuals, often insensitive to feelings; shows partiality | Attempts to grow in understanding and acceptance rapport | Demonstrates equal acceptance of all abilities; easily approached; supports the self-confidence of children |

Staff	Harmonious relationships; friendly; respected; shares and discusses ideas and knowledge; consults with other professional personnel	Usually maintains positive working relationship with staff	Limits contact with other staff members; hesitates to share and discuss ideas
Parents	Reluctantly responds to parent contacts; has difficulty establishing rapport; misinterprets policy	Confers willingly; does not always communicate effetively	Seeks to confer with parents; is articulate in interpreting school policies and practices
Atmosphere Climate	Little evidence of pupils and teacher working together	Some evidence of pupils and teacher working and planning together; orderly, purposeful	Self-discipline; attitude of respect and cooperation; uniqueness of individuals is valued

PRINCIPAL'S COMMENTS:

Figure 2. Statement Concerning Work of Teacher and Recommendation for Re-Employment, Minneapolis Public Schools, Department of Personnel.

Fig. 2, continued

II. PERSONAL QUALITIES

Knowledge of Subject	Makes errors of fact; has inadequate background	Knowledge is sufficient for most situations; tends to favor topics he knows most about	Educated in depth; rich background beyond present needs; continues to learn
Sense of Humor	Keen sense of humor; uses it to relieve tension	Readily perceives humor; uses humor to hold interest	Occasionally uses humor; unresponsive in humorous situations
Initiative	Does perfunctory job; routine	Secures ideas from others; tries them out	Creative in solving problems; has experimental attitude; goes beyond requirements of job
Enthusiasm	Apathetic, depresses enthusiasm in others	Occasionally rises to accept and explore interesting ideas and events	Zestful, seeks new ideas and approaches and arouses enthusiasm in others
Poise	Self-assured, calm, mature; controls emotions	Occasionally annoyed by events and relationships; generally able	Easily moved to anger or depression; insecure

12

Voice Diction	Unusual clarity of speech; high level of word choice; flexible use of volume, pitch, tone	"English" is generally satisfactory; uses appropriately to situation	Distracting vocal mannerisms, or poor English usage
Judgment	Self-reliant; reasons clearly; sees long term effect of his actions	Usually responds to crises intelligently; seeks advisement on complex problems if necessary	Makes hasty decisions; does not perceive effects of actions, does not seek advice
Attitudes	Satisfied with present status. Is offended by suggestions. Seldom seeks new methods or techniques	Accepts suggestions. Modifies practices to some extent	Exceptionally alert to new trends and techniques. Shares ideas with others. Seeks suggestions

PRINCIPAL'S COMMENTS:

13

Fig. 2, *continued*

III. LEARNING ACTIVITIES

Planning	Has flexible plan; provides for the individual differences. Aims for total involvement of all pupils	Shows evidences of pre-planning. Purpose is evident; lesson is sequential and logical	Shows confusion about what to do and where to begin
Motivation	Uses student interests, needs and experiences as a springboard	Blends extrinsic and intrinsic motivation	Lacking or inadequate; uses externally imposed motivation entirely
Development and Continuity	Treats important concepts vaguely. Needs to build pupil readiness and awareness of purpose	Moves in an orderly manner through sequence of lesson. Occasionally seeks student feedback as means of checking progress of child	Moves to succeeding parts of lesson as a result of pupil comprehension. Moves to a point of summary and evaluation. Aims for "discovery" and inductive learning
Sensitivity to Individual Differences	Assumes all children learn at the same rate. Lacks knowledge of individual pupils	Knows of the individual strengths and weaknesses of each child. Seeks information on behavior problems	Shows insight into the developmental level of all children and applies this knowledge when working with the individual child
Uses of Various Resources, Aids, Instructional Materials	Uses a wide variety of appropriate materials. Seeks to improve them	Usually supplements textbook to some extent. Fair incorporation	Uses textbook only

14

Use of Various Instructional Techniques and Methods	Uses one technique exclusively	Uses a different technique or method occasionally	Varies the technique and method with the individual individual capacities and expectations
Lesson Outcome- Knowledge, Skills and Attitudes	Sees knowledge and skills as the end result. Knowledge and skills are not related to problem. Overlooking opportunity for potential learning	Well developed content and skills but little transfers to more significant questions	Knowledge and skills are functionally used in solving problem or in the development of attitudes
Physical Environment	Orderly and attractive; pupils contribute to the order and attractiveness; functional seating arrangements	Shows some attention to interest but lacks some organization	Disorderly, uninteresting

PRINCIPAL'S COMMENTS:

15

Fig. 2, *continued*

PRINCIPAL'S SUMMARY STATEMENT

This evaluation is based on _____ visits to the teacher's classroom _____ conferences.

COMMENTS:

CLASSROOM VISITS
Date	Length of time

CONFERENCES
Date	Length of time

The re-employment of this teacher is approved _____ disapproved _____
*approved with reservation _____
*This applies to first and second year of probation only.

Date _____ Signed _____ Principal

Teacher's Comments:

Date: _____ Signed: _____ Teacher

For additonal comments use a separate page.
Teacher's signature indicates that he/she has seen the above statement.

The re-employment of this teacher is approved _____ disapproved _____

Date: _____   Signed: _____
                                      Associate Superintendent

The re-employment of this teacher is approved _____ disapproved _____

Date: _____   Signed: _____
                                      Superintendent

17

EVALUATION OF TEACHING

Name _____ Date _____

Teaching Situation _____

Learning Activity _____

I.   Assessment

     A. Informal

     B. Formal

II. Planning

     A. Selecting objectives

     B. Devising and sequencing learning activities

III. Teaching

     A. Clear to pupil(s)

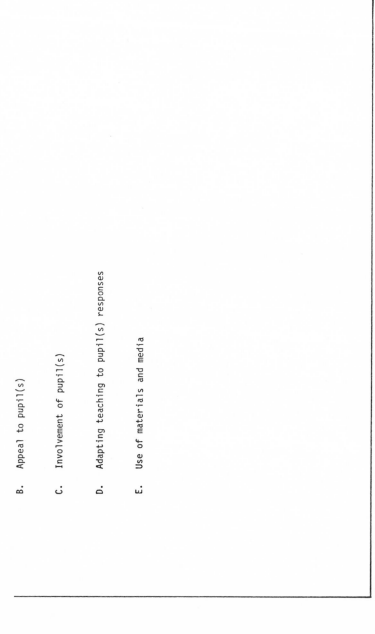

B.   Appeal to pupil(s)

C.   Involvement of pupil(s)

D.   Adapting teaching to pupil(s) responses

E.   Use of materials and media

Figure 3. Evaluation of Teaching Form, Temple University, Department of Special Education.

20

Fig. 3, *continued*

Evaluation of Teaching
Page 2

III. Teaching (Cont.)

    F.   Provision of opportunity for practice and reinforcement

    G.   Classroom and pupil management

IV. Conferring and Consulting

V.   Evaluation

COMMENTS

MONTHLY PERFORMANCE RATING

Failure (F)   Marginal Quality (C)   Satisfactory Quality (B)   Superior Quality (A)

Signature:

Student _____

Supervisor _____

Table 1. Categories of Observation Systems in Simon and Boyer, *Mirrors for Behavior: An Anthology of Observation Instruments,* (1974).

	Affective	Cognitive	Psychomotor (body movement)	Activity	Procedure for routine content	Sociological structure	Physical environment	Other
1. Amidon (MCS)	X	X						
2. Amidon-Hunter (VICS)	X							
3. Aschner-Gallagher		X		X	X			
4. Bellack		X			X			
5. Flanders (FSIA)	X							
6. Flanders (Expanded)	X	X		X				
7. Gallagher		X		X		X		
8. Honigman (MACI)	X			X	X			
9. Hough	X			X				
10. Houges	X		X	X	X			
11. Joyce	X	X			X			
12. Lindvall				X				
13. Medley (Oscar 4V)	X	X		X	X	X	X	
14. Miller	X	X						
15. Moskowitz (Flint)	X							
16. Oliver-Shaver	X	X	X	X	X			
17. Openshaw-Cyphert	X	X			X			
18. Simon-Agazarian (SAVI)		X				X		
19. Smith (Logic)		X				X		
20. Smith (Strategies)		X						

#	Author/System	1	2	3	4	5	6	7
21.	Spaulding (Cases)	X	X				X	
22.	Spaulding (Stars)	X	X		X		X	
23.	Taba	X	X		X			
24.	Withall	X				X		
25.	Wright	X						X
26.	Wright-Proctor	X	X		X		X	
27.	Adams-Biddle	X	X		X	X	X	
28.	Altman	X	X		X			
29.	Anderson, A.	X	X				X	
30.	Anderson, H. H.	X		X		X		
31.	Argyris	X	X				X	
32.	Bales	X	X		X		X	
33.	Barnes	X	X		X			
34.	Blumberg	X						
35.	Borgatta (BSs)	X				X	X	
36.	Brown (TPOR)		X		X	X		
37.	Brown et al. (FTCB)		X		X			
38.	Buehler-Richmond			X		X	X	
39.	Clements		X					
40.	C.E.R.L.I. (CVC)	X	X	X		X	X	
41.	Denny-Rusch-Ives (CCOS)	X	X		X		X	
42.	DODL	X	X					
43.	Fuller (Fair 33)	X		X	X			X
44.	Galloway	X					X	
45.	Hall		X			X		

Table 1, *continued*

	Affective	Cognitive	Psychomotor (body movement)	Activity	Procedure for routine content	Sociological structure	Physical environment	Other
46. Herbert (SAL)	X	X	X	X		X	X	X
47. Hill (HIM)	X					X	X	X
48. Homigman-Stephens (SAP)	X	X		X			X	
49. Hunter	X	X					X	
50. Jansen	X			X	X			
51. Jason (MIOR)	X			X				
52. Kowatrakul	X	X	X	X				X
53. Longabaugh (R-P)	X	X	X		X	X		
54. MacDonald-Zaret								
55. Matthews—Teacher (SCAS)	X		X	X		X		X
56. Matthews—Student (SCAS)	X			X		X		
57. Melbin	X			X	X	X		
58. McRel (MIA)		X			X			
59. Mills (SPA)	X					X		
60. Moustakas—Sigel Schalock	X			X	X	X		

	1	2	3	4	5	6	7
61. Ober (RCS)	X	X					
62. Parakh (PBCS)	X	X				X	X
63. Perkins (Teacher)	X	X			X		
64. Perkins (Student)	X	X		X			
65. Ribble-Schultz	X	X				X	
66. Riskin	X	X		X	X		
67. Robertson	X	X		X	X		
68. Roberts	X	X		X	X		
69. Schalock (TR)	X	X		X	X	X	X
70. Schusler (CIMAR)	X	X		X	X	X	X
71. Snyder	X	X					
72. Solomon (TIP)	X	X					
73. Steinzor	X	X					
74. Stukat-Engstrom	X	X		X	X	X	
75. Tyler	X	X		X	X		X
76. Waimon	X	X		X	X	X	
77. Wallen et al. (Stepos)	X	X		X	X		
78. Withall-Lewis-Newell	X	X		X	X		
79. WRAGG	X						

routine. The *sociological structure* category deal with the roles of the people who are interacting. For instance, if a distinction is made between the teacher and pupils, then the system would be rated in this category. The last category, *physical environment,* describes the physical setting and the specific materials which are unique to the observation.

Upon examination of Table 1, one notices that observation systems may be rated in more than one of the seven categories, as shown in the Table. It is clear from the extensive list of observation models that researchers have been experimenting in ways by which teaching behavior can be validly defined, quantified, and studied. Various systems of interaction analysis have been developed to study the relationship between teacher and pupils.

Flander's (1970) Interaction Analysis

One such system is that developed by Ned Flanders (1970), which is concerned with verbal behavior. The objective of this system is to provide teachers with the opportunity to study their own behavior in a systematic, objective manner so as to change behavior. Effective classroom verbal behavior is an important skill in teaching. It is based on the assumption that the verbal behavior of an individual is representative of his/her total behavior (Amidon and Flanders, 1971).

Categories within Model All statements that occur in the classroom are categorized into three sections:

1. Teacher talk
2. Pupil talk
3. Silence, confusion, or other

Teacher verbal behavior is then subdivided into direct and indirect statements. Direct statements are, in the words of Amidon and Flanders, those that "minimize the freedom of the student to respond." Indirect statements "maximize the freedom of the student to respond." *Teacher-indirect statements* include those that:

1. Accept feeling
2. Praise or encourage

3. Accept ideas
4. Ask questions

Teacher-direct statements are those that:

1. Lecture
2. Give directions
3. Criticize or justify authority

Pupil talk includes:

1. Responding to the teacher
2. Initiating talk

Silence, confusion, or other encompasses those times when it is difficult to determine who is talking.

Method of Recording   An observer records the interplay between teacher and pupils. Every 3 seconds the observer writes down the category number of the interaction just observed. The numbers are recorded in sequence and then entered on matrix which can be analyzed in terms of behavior patterns.

Evaluation of Model   Flander's interaction analysis provides feedback concerning teacher performance and allows teachers to practice the behavior to be changed. The system allows for data to be systematically and objectively collected. Another advantage of this system is that supervisors can have a graphic representation of the teaching act and can easily point out strengths and weaknesses. The system represents a significant step forward toward objectivity and minimizing subjective supervisor opinion. However, it is limited to verbal behavior and does not reflect antecedent versus consequence characteristics needed to evaluate classroom management skills.

DEVELOPMENT OF OBSERVATION SYSTEMS EMPLOYING BEHAVIORAL PRINCIPLES

Identifying Effective Teaching Behavior

Classroom observation systems were originally designed for research purposes. Subsequently, they have been used as a means of training teachers and evaluating their classroom behavior. Identifying effective classroom behavior has been not only the most difficult, but the most crucial issue of the process. Determining what is considered "good" teaching behavior has been the major difficulty. The tenets of individualizing instruction and systematic use of contingencies (behavioral principles) have become the accepted and desired teaching behaviors to be exhibited in the classroom (Brown and York, 1974; Haring, 1977; Peter, 1972; Tucker and Horner, 1977). Therefore, supervisors have become increasingly interested in training and observing teachers using those techniques.

Diagnostic-Prescriptive Approach

Individualizing instruction, also referred to as the diagnostic-prescriptive approach (Haring, 1977; Peter, 1972; Tucker and Horner, 1977) includes:

1. Assessing a pupil's present level of functioning through formal or informal procedures
2. Writing a terminal objective describing the result of the instruction
3. Sequencing instructional steps to achieve the objective
4. Determining a means of measuring or recording progress

It is also recommended that a pupil's specific strengths and weaknesses be considered when setting up an individualized program of instruction (Mann and Suiter, 1974).

Behavioral Objective Writing

Mager (1962) is responsible for the organization and general acceptance of behavioral objective writing in education today. Since objectives are useful tools in designing, implementing, and evaluating instruction, they are utilized in both regular and special education programs. Objective writing has paved the way for programmed materials in all instructional areas—reading, math, social studies, etc. (Harris and Smith, 1972). Materials like the Sullivan Reading Series (Buchanen, 1968) and Systems 80 (Durrell, 1973) utilize behavioral objectives and the sequencing of small teaching steps. Special education accentuates the importance of the diagnostic-prescriptive approach with the enactment of Education for All Handicapped Children Act of 1975 (P.L. 94-142). It is mandated that an Individual Education Program (IEP) be designed for each handicapped child. The IEP is a statement which includes the following:

1. Present level of educational level of performance
2. Annual long and short term goals and objectives
3. Specific education services to be provided and extent to which the child will remain in regular education
4. Projected initiation and duration of services
5. Objective criteria or evaluation procedures to determine progress of the child in meeting the goals

Therefore, supervisors and teacher trainers have become increasingly interested in observing and evaluating teachers in their use of behavioral objective writing when individualizing instruction. (Chapter 4 presents a detailed account of the elements of good behavioral objective writing.)

Use of Principles of Behavior Management

How They Work   As individualizing instruction has become an undisputed part of "good" teaching, so has the use of behavioral principles. Behavior, in the classroom, refers to both academic and social performance. Specifically, the behaviors with which most teachers are concerned include:

1. Completing reading and math assignments
2. Answering questions posed by the teacher
3. Sitting still
4. Raising one's hand in class

According to Axelrod (1977), the occurrence of these behaviors is influenced by the positive or negative events or consequences which follow the behaviors. *If the consequence which follows a behavior is positive, it increases the likelihood that the behavior will occur again.* For example, if a student is called on to answer a question after raising his/her hand, chances are that the hand-raising behavior will occur again when the student desires to answer the next time. Hand raising in class is viewed as the desired behavior while calling on the student whose hand is raised is the positive consequence. In order for consequences to have maximum effect, they must be used in a contingent manner. A *contingent relationship* is defined as one in which the consequence that a student receives depends on the behavior which occurs. In other words, it is an "if/then" relationship. "If the student completes all of his/her written assignments, then he/she may go outside for recess." Contingencies are to be used in a systematic manner.

Applications to Classroom Situations   According to Hall (in Axelrod, 1977), the use of behavioral principles in the classroom has allowed teachers to deal with both academic and social management problems more directly and effectively. Axelrod (1977) and O'Leary and O'Leary (1972) cite numerous studies where principles of behavior management have been systematically applied to classroom situations. Data have been collected to determine their effectiveness. Studies have also been conducted to determine if training in the use of contingencies has been successful (*e.g.,* Becker, Madsen, Arnold and Thomas, 1967).

Teacher Training in Behavioral Management Principles Hall, Panyon, Rabon, and Broden (1968) conducted a study in which three first-year teachers who were experiencing difficulty in controlling classroom behavior were trained to use systematic reinforcement procedures. Before training was instituted, an observer recorded pupil and teacher behavior over a period of several days. The observer recorded each pupil's behavior twice on a consecutive rotating basis for a 10-second interval, (or 5-second, in one case). If the particular pupil was exhibiting nonstudy behavior (i.e., out of seat, talking out of turn, etc.) any time during the interval, "N" for nonstudy behavior was recorded. If the pupil was attending or behaving appropriately, then "S" for study behavior was recorded. The percentage of study time for the entire class was computed by dividing the number of study intervals by the total number of observation intervals and multiplying by 100. The observer also analyzed teacher behavior by recording verbalizations: a "+" was recorded if a teacher's comment followed an appropriate pupil study behavior; a "−" was recorded if the comment followed a pupil nonstudy behavior. It was found that, in general, those comments following appropriate pupil study behavior were positive in nature whereas those following inappropriate behavior were in the form of a reprimand. Training consisted of an explanation of reinforcement procedures. The teacher was instructed to increase the frequency of positive comments following appropriate study behavior. After each observation session, the results of teacher and pupil behavior were shared with the teacher. For one of the teachers, training and feedback were sufficient to increase classroom control. The other two teachers used an additional contingency to achieve desired control. The results of this study indicated that supervisors and principals could train new teachers to use reinforcement procedures, thereby increasing classroom effectiveness.

According to Ringer (1973), most training in applying learning principles to the classroom centers around formal teacher instruction. Ringer suggests that an alternative means of training would be actually to model the desired teaching techniques for the teacher in his/her own classroom. It is his belief that this type of training decreases the need for verbal explanations and conveys the technique more easily and more vividly. The intent of this study was to train the classroom teacher to use a token reinforcement program by modeling the desired techniques. The token reinforcement program consisted of pairing verbal praise with the trainer's initialing a card which was placed on each pupil's desk. During the academic session the trainer or "token helper" moved around the room initialing cards of those pupils about whom the teacher made positive comments concerning their appropriate behavior. The teacher gradually assumed more and more of the responsibility for initialing the cards and for providing the positive reinforcement. Through the use of a modeling technique, the "token helper" was able to train the teacher. Results of the study indicated that the teacher was able to decrease disruptive behavior using a token reinforcement program which was modeled by the trainer.

Need for Supervision in Training Process

Horton (1975) commented that a major problem which supervisors and teacher trainers face is the management of the actual training process so that appropriate teacher behavior can be initiated, maintained, and generalized to all subject areas and situations. In his study, Horton trained two teachers to praise pupils by identifying the specific student behavior and attaching a series of words which connotates approval (*i.e.,* "You read that sentence correctly, Mary."). Training included the use of videotapes and audiotapes as feedback mechanisms as well as verbal instruction in the use of praise. Results showed that the rate of teacher praise increased with training. However, the training and subsequent use of behavior-specific praise in one subject or content area did not produce the behavior in other areas where the training was not given.

Results of the studies cited indicate that teachers can learn to manage the academic and social behaviors in their classrooms more effectively through various training procedures. However, there still remains a need to more systematically record "good" teaching behaviors, including individualizing instruction and managing behavior. An assessment procedure is needed to allow supervisors to evaluate their effectiveness in the classroom. The data collected must be in the form of discrete and observable events. Subjective information must be minimized or eliminated. A means of formally documenting all observable and measurable behaviors involved in individualizing instruction and managing classroom behavior is essential.

In order for teachers to be adequately trained, supervision must be available not only in pre-service programs, but in in-service ones as well. Teachers need opportunities to practice their newly learned skills and to receive feedback so that they realize whether their behavior is appropriate or not. Old skills must be refined and new skills should be incorporated into a teaching repertoire. Only through close supervision will the quality of teaching improve, thus increasing the likelihood that pupil performance will increase as well.

Chapter 2
Measurement of Teacher Rapport

RATIONALE FOR TECHNIQUE

The most perplexing, difficult, and delicate problem related to supervision is that of providing feedback regarding variables that have to do with the teacher's personality. In this area, especially, it would be desirable to be objective so as to avoid personal judgments on the part of the supervisor altogether. How do you tell the teacher that he or she is flat or boring, hostile toward the children, inconsistent, or insensitive to student needs? In the past, such comments were likely to be taken as personal insults and the supervisor-teacher relationship would be seriously damaged. There is little the supervisor can do to support or improve a teacher's skills after such an encounter. Therefore, supervisors typically avoid this area altogether, despite the fact that teacher, supervisor, parent, and student would all readily admit to the importance of what will be called the "rapport skills." If these skills can, at least in part, be measured in an objective manner, then the supersensitive subject can again be approached. The supervisor would then no longer act as the decision maker or evaluator regarding the desirability of the teacher's personality.

Rather, the supervisor becomes a feedback agent in terms of what the teacher has done during the observations. Given a sufficient understanding of the feedback mechanism, it is possible for the teacher to make his or her own evaluations of the data with no, or minimal, direction from the supervisor. Two fundamental questions arise: 1) with feedback, does the behavior of teachers change, and 2) can "teacher rapport" be accurately measured?

Does the Behavior of Teachers Change with Feedback?

Supervisory experiences at both pre-service and in-service levels leave little doubt that teachers can change if given frequent and objective data on specific variables. Research regarding social interaction and dating back to studies of teacher behavior by Becker, Madsen, Arnold, and Thomas (1967) further confirm the contention that variables commonly associated with the somewhat vague term of "personality" can and do change. Pre-service students in several teacher training programs in the Temple University Department of Special Education, as well as several neighboring supervisory units of working teachers, keep on-going records of teacher behavior and consistently demonstrate that most teachers change readily if given objective feedback regarding well defined variables.

Can "Teacher Rapport" Be Accurately Measured?

By implication, the question is already answered. There must be variables that can be defined and measured. After many hours of searching for intelligent suggestions with a group of generally outstanding supervisors, it was concluded that the behavioral aspects of good rapport might best be measured according to *how the teacher behaves in response to the behaviors of children.* That is, rapport is a function of how the teacher responds to what students do. We further agreed that the way teachers in "good rapport" respond to children should be generally positive, appropriate, and consistent. In observing the changes in children when these values are imposed, there is little doubt that they are desirable descriptors. A paper describing the supervisory system was presented to an audience of over 100 educators at a national teacher's convention (CEC, Chicago, 1976). As an additional confirmation of the values underlying the system, the audience concurred with them unanimously.

DEVELOPMENT OF THE INSTRUMENT

The next step was to design a system[1] in which teacher responses to the behaviors of their students could be categorized in such a way that they would reflect the degree to which the teacher's behavior was *positive, appropriate,* and *consistent.* When a teacher made a response fitting the definition of a category, a slash mark (/) was entered on the form. Two categories of responses were most obvious (positive and negative), with a third for those in between (neutral). Experiences as a school psychologist, teacher, and teacher-trainer suggested that these three simplistic categories were insufficient.

The value of being *positive,* without additional complexity, would suggest that only positive responses are needed. Yet a teacher cannot say "very good" to a spelling error, or "Terrific!" when a child destroys his neighbor's paper. The teacher must also be *appropriate.* That is, *positive responses should follow appropriate behavior and negative responses should follow inappropriate behaviors.* To be positive, then, the teacher must make the former response more often than the latter, or she must catch them being good more often than being bad. On the assumption that most students are rewarded by attention, neutral or in-between responses were originally scored as positive. To that point, there were four defined categories:

1. Positive to appropriate behavior
2. Positive to inappropriate behavior
3. Negative to appropriate behavior
4. Negative to inappropriate behavior

---

[1]The completed form, as it was finally established, appears on pages 46, 47 (Figure 4). The same form, with hypothetical entries, appears on pages 50–55 (Figures 5–7). You may wish to refer to these as you read this chapter.

Consistency, the third value, requires the teacher to be predictable in response to certain behavior. Applied to the categories, the implication is that the teacher should be positive only to appropriates and negative only to inappropriates.

Academic Versus Social Behavior

The four-category system was a beginning, but it was too general. Teachers who were known to be significantly different in rapport from a subjective point of view and who were very different in ability to control a class or maintain a positive atmosphere were too often identical on the observation categories. More was needed to discriminate the near ideal from the not-so-near. After many observations, it was noticed that teachers as a whole differed less in their responses to academic tasks than in their responses to social behaviors. Only a very few teachers, those generally considered the best, took the time to attend to students because they were behaving well, whereas nearly every teacher gave a positive response to a correct academic response. By separating the behavior the students performed into *academic* (direct response to the curriculum) *behavior* versus *social behavior* and by maintaining the four categories for each kind of behavior, the observation form was expanded to include eight categories, four social and four academic. The observer must be able to discriminate between social and academic behaviors easily. Academic behaviors are those in direct response to the curriculum such as solving problems, answering questions, oral reading, and spelling. Social behaviors are less related to the curriculum than to following classroom rules or routines. Often included are such behaviors as hand raising (even if in response to an academic question), task completion within certain limits, remaining in a seat, standing in line, waiting a turn, shouting out, and a whole host of disruptive or off-task behaviors. Observations now began to discriminate between teachers. They were no longer all alike and, more important, certain patterns of responding corresponded to subjective ratings of the teachers' rapport.

Academic Response

The Corrective   There were still too often responses that were difficult to place. Many teachers provide a sort of positive and negative simultaneously in response to an academic error as in the example, "No, but almost. Try again." Teachers, supervisors, teacher-trainers, and administrators have all agreed that this response is superior to the negative, "No, the answer is _____." A fifth category was added to the response to academic behavior column and was labeled *corrective*. There is an endless number of ways a teacher can supply a corrective, but to be a corrective, the teacher's response must be neutral or positive in tone and allow the student the opportunity to correct his or her error. In the corrective, the teacher may simply pause to suggest to the student something like "No, that wasn't it. You'd better try another response," or the teacher may supply additional information such as the initial sound of a difficult word, or direct the student to a problem-solving strategy. The teacher may go so far as to model the correct response so that the student can repeat it.

Ignoring Incorrects and Ignoring Corrects   To account for all responses to academic behaviors, there was a need for two more categories: *ignoring incorrects* and *ignoring corrects*. There are often times when the material presented is largely review in nature. In this case skilled teachers often listen to a series, sometimes quite lengthy, of responses before indicating that they were correct. The technique is highly functional in that it consumes no time and the lack of a corrective implies, in almost every classroom, that the response was correct.

Because of the implication of "correct if ignored" regarding an academic response, *ignoring an incorrect is generally misleading and should be avoided as an error in giving feedback*. For example, if the child responds incorrectly to a multiplication flash card and the teacher goes on to the next card without a corrective, the student will have been lead to believe an incorrect multiplication fact.

Identifying Creative and/or Enthusiastic Teachers After extensive field testing, only one addition to academic responses seemed necessary to establish the basic construct validity of high positive correlation between the supervisor's subjective reaction to the teacher's rapport and the observational tool. There was a need to subdivide the "positive to a correct academic response" category. Entries made in the upper half of the category indicate an enthusiastic, novel, or otherwise highly rewarding positive. Entries in the lower half represent knowledge-of-results kinds of responses such as "OK," "ugh-huh," "good," or repetition of the correct response. The addition was found to be necessary to identify enthusiastic and creative teachers who maintain interest in their feedback from teachers who may give positive feedback at appropriate times, but who are rather uninteresting, or who may use the same positive so repetitiously that it may become ineffective for or even offensive to some students.

Enough Is Enough The temptation to keep adding more categories to gain more detailed records must be avoided. The observation instrument can quickly become too complex to be readily usable. If both the teacher and the observer do not fully understand the record, its function will be largely lost. For pragmatic reasons, then, the categories under responses to academic behaviors were not broken down further. In instances when it may seem desirable to do so, modification can be made easily. One common example is the case where the observer notices a strong predisposition to respond to certain children over others in a group situation. The supervisor may enter different symbols for responses to certain children as in the case of an "X" rather than a slash mark ("/"). Again, caution must be exercised to avoid complexities that make interpretations difficult.

Social Response

Need for Teacher Training The final developments in the instrument regarding the social response may appear far more parallel than they actually are. It was repeatedly found that nearly all teachers responded correctly to academic responses with little or no training. The opposite was found repeatedly for social behavior. Given many children in a classroom setting, it seems natural for most untrained adults to notice only inappropriate social behavior. These behaviors may be more attention getting, so much so that appropriate social behaviors are ignored entirely. The tendency gives rise to several problems.

Attention-Getting Devices Many students crave attention of any kind. When attention is received most reliably and most immediately with inappropriate behavior, these behaviors may quickly accelerate until the teaching-learning process is severely disturbed.

Law of Decelerating Consequences The most basic principles of learning theory require that *an inappropriate behavior should be followed by a decelerating consequence.* In effect, the teacher, by attending only to socially inappropriate behaviors, may find it necessary to be uncomfortably negative or punitive. Although punitive responses may well be called for, they should be counterbalanced by several positives for appropriate social behavior.

Pressure To Be Positive The matter is further complicated by a pervasive pressure felt by all teachers, and imposed by the students, parents, other teachers, administrators, and the system at large, to give positive responses. This pressure, coupled with attending to only inappropriate social behaviors, may give rise to a host of errors. Observation of hundreds of teachers bears this difficulty out; inappropriate social behaviors are commonly followed by positive teacher responses both in affective tone and in the linguistic content of the response.

The Solution The solution to all of these difficulties is easily stated, but often very difficult for individual teachers. The teacher must notice children behaving appropriately as well as inappropriately: "Catch them being good, and do so more often than you catch them being bad."

Social Behavior Categories *Positive Response—To Appropriate Social Behavior* On the Social behavior side of the chart in figure 4, the *positive response to appropriate social behavior* becomes an extremely important category. The teacher has an opportunity to give a positive tone to the classroom atmosphere by freely using this category whenever appropriate.

Positive Response—Appropriate to Orient One Off-Task The second category, *appropriate to orient one off-task,* similarly requires the teacher to attend positively to appropriate social behavior, but with an added complication. The attention in this case, although reinforcing for the on-task child, is designed to reorient someone who is off-task. In this way, children who begin to wander from their work can be reminded to get back to it without giving them attention directly. The category amounts to the identification of appropriate peer models. For example:

> John and Bill are friends. John is working, but Bill is daydreaming or wandering about the class. The teacher says, "I really like the way Mary, Sara, George, and John are still working hard!" Bill, assuming he's bright enough to be socially aware, will be reminded to get back to work.

The technique is rarely used, but is surprisingly effective in most classes. To convince the doubtful teacher, the teacher is asked to leave the classroom until the noise level begins to escalate. Then the teacher is instructed to reenter the room and name and praise children who are still, or nearly still, at work. Order is usually reestablished at a rate that will surprise and impress most teachers.

Positive Response—To Inappropriate Social Behavior The third category calls for the teacher to *respond positively to inappropriate social behavior,* the common error referred to earlier. A child may tear up his math paper and the teacher may approach the child and ask him what else he'd rather do, or send the child to a very pleasant and supportive counselor, or to a high interest area—consequences that should follow task completion rather than task destruction.

Corrective Category After months of field testing, supervisors reported that neutrally stated corrections of off-task behaviors, such as "Mary, sit down please," were difficult to score as positives to inappropriates. The teachers protested as well. The initial rationalization that attention, unless clearly negative in nature, functions as a positive reward for many children was abandoned. The neutral *corrective* for inappropriate social behaviors was established. A small number of these responses over a 20-minute observation session is probably not of much importance. If the proportion of correctives is high relative to the total number of responses to social behaviors, there is a problem. The teacher is spending too much time telling students, who probably already know what to do, what to do. It would imply that the students either enjoy the attention or might be attempting to slow down curricular presentations. The teacher, in such a case, is probably well advised to identify and reward peer models instead.

Ignoring Response—To Inappropriate and Appropriate Social Behaviors The next two categories include instances of *ignoring inappropriate social behaviors* and *ignoring appropriate social behaviors*. Unimportant inappropriate behaviors can often be ignored, and if ignored consistently as in an extinction procedure, may significantly decrease, especially if incompatible on-task behaviors are rewarded. It is consistency that is of utmost importance in extinction procedures. The minimally negative component of the strategy makes it a highly desirable procedure for many minor misbehaviors.

It would be disruptive and too difficult to attend to all appropriate social behaviors. There are too many. Yet any student who is on-task longer than is usual for that student deserves some recognition and appreciation. Entries are recorded in this category in regard to specific behaviors or specific students whom the teacher has beforehand identified as problematic.

Negative Response—To Inappropriate and Appropriate Social Behavior The last two categories are *negative response to inappropriate social behavior* and *negative response to appropriate social behavior*. Unless the teacher has an unusually sarcastic disposition, the latter is rarely recorded. The error involved is too obvious and training is almost always unnecessary. The former, negatives to inappropriates, is the more important. Some inappropriate behavior, that which is dangerous to others or to significant property and that which is excessively disruptive, forces the teacher to attend. Because the behavior is clearly inappropriate, the teacher's response should be one that will reduce its frequency. The response should be unquestionably negative and effective; times like these do not call for half-hearted responses. Of course, the teacher must use alternatives that are acceptable to the system and full control over emotional reaction is always necessary. *A good rule of thumb is to find at least five positives to attend to for each negative.* In this way, a positive atmosphere will be preserved and the contrast between positive and negative will be accentuated. The negative response will more likely have the appropriate effect on the behavior.

FINAL ORGANIZATION OF RAPPORT OBSERVATION FORM (TEACHER RESPONSE TO STUDENT BEHAVIOR)

The final organization of the rapport observation form (Teacher Response to Student Behavior) appears in Figure 4 (pages 46 and 47). Teacher responses to academic behaviors are recorded on the left half, responses to social behaviors on the right half. Entries are made in each category as they occur, usually as slash marks (/). Space for a description of the on-going classroom activity and the number of students involved is at the left-hand margin as well as space for recording the exact time of the observation.

The blank lines separating columns are to provide space for notetaking in regard to the responses recorded in categories to the left of the lines. Especially when errors are made, the supervisor is well advised to write enough to be able to recall the specific incident. Teachers are not likely to believe certain errors without more detailed information. In an analogous way, notes should be taken when a teacher does something unusually well, so that the supervisor can provide appropriate praise or reinforcement.

SUMMARY AND REVIEW OF
TEACHER RESPONSE TO STUDENT BEHAVIOR FORM

Academic Behavior Responses

To review the form, all responses recorded are those of the teacher to what children do. Responses to academic performances are entered on the left. When the teacher makes a very positive, creative, or otherwise especially rewarding response, it is entered in the top left category *(1)*. Responses that provide simple knowledge of correct responses, but which are not affectively loaded, are entered in the second to the top left *(2)*. Responses that are positive to incorrect responses are entered in the third to the top left category *(3)*. In instances where the child errs and the teacher communicates the erroneous nature of the response, but in a positive to neutral tone, then provides the opportunity for the student to correct her/himself, the response is an academic corrective *(4)*. Responses that constitute ignoring the student's response (as when the teacher proceeds to the next item or question without comment), are entered under ignoring incorrect if the student's response was incorrect *(5),* or ignoring correct if the student's response was correct *(6)*. Negative responses to academic behaviors are recorded in the last categories on the left *(7, 8)*. The response may be minimally negative as is the case of neutrally telling a student he/she is incorrect without a corrective component, or the response may be affectively negative as well. If the student's response is incorrect, the negative teacher response is recorded in the second from the bottom category *(7)*. If the student's response is correct, the negative teacher response is entered on the bottom left category *(8)*.

Social Behavior Responses

Responses to social behaviors are recorded on the right-hand side of the form. Positive responses to appropriate behaviors are recorded in the first or top category of the column *(9)*. Similar responses, but in instances where the observer believes that the

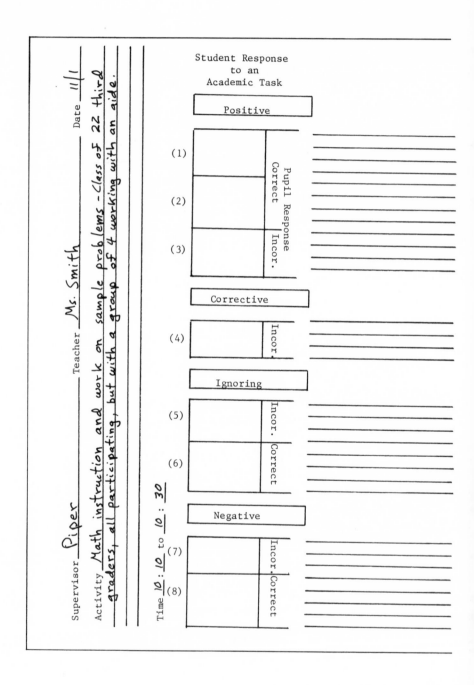

Supervisor _Piper_   Teacher _Ms. Smith_   Date _11/1_

Activity _Math instruction and work on sample problems - Class of 22 third_
graders, all participating, but with a group of 4 working with an aide.

Time _10_ : _10_ to _10_ : _30_

Student Response
to an
Academic Task

Positive

(1)

(2)   Pupil Response
                       Correct   Incor.
(3)

Corrective

(4)   Incor.

Ignoring

(5)   Incor.   Correct

(6)

Negative

(7)   Incor. Correct

(8)

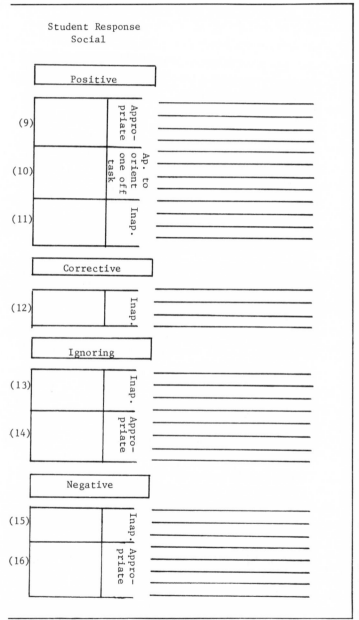

Figure 4. Teacher Response to Student Behavior Form.

teacher's response was designed to remind other off-task children to get back to task, are recorded in the second category *(10)*. The third category is for recording instances of positive responses to inappropriate social behavior *(11)*. When the teacher tells children what they should be doing in response to their off-task behavior, but the teacher's tone or words are not noticeably positive or negative, the response is recorded as a social corrective, the fourth social category *(12)*. Ignoring inappropriate or appropriate social behaviors is recorded in the fifth and sixth categories, respectively *(13, 14)*. Since social behaviors are continually on-going and the teacher cannot respond to all or even most of them, entries are typically limited to particular behaviors of teacher or supervisor concern. Negative responses to social behaviors always have negative affective tone or disapproval. (Negative statements made neutrally such as "Stop that, Mary" should be entered under social corrective). When the negatives are to inappropriate social behaviors, they are recorded in the seventh category *(15)*. When the child's behavior is appropriate, and the teacher responds negatively, an entry is made in the eighth or last category *(16)*.

IDEAL PATTERNS

In instructional situations where a teacher is actively responding to a class, an interaction pattern will become discernible on the observation form after a short period of time. Fifteen or 20 minutes is generally adequate to develop this pattern. The preceding description of categories has implied that some patterns are highly desirable and that some constitute errors.

In effect, there are highly desirable overall patterns of responding as well as undesirable patterns, and these patterns will emerge on the form. Figures 5, 6, and 7 are provided as examples of these patterns. Figure 5 (pages 50, 51) is an example of a well trained teacher's recording; Figure 6 (pages 52, 53) represents a more typical, perhaps partially trained teacher; and Figure 7 (pages 54, 55) shows a teacher who needs a great deal of training. Notice that the well trained teacher in Figure 5 relies, almost exclusively, upon "catching children being good." This teacher takes advantage of opportunities to praise. There is consistency, appropriateness, and an overall positive pattern. On the other hand, the teacher in Figure 7 tends to concentrate attention on errors. Although not often inappropriate, there will certainly be a threatening, military-like atmosphere in such a class.

There are modifications possible on the ideal that are a function of:

1. The level of functioning of the student
2. The lesson
3. Specific behaviors that may be occurring

Only relative frequencies can be specified because of variations in class size, personalities of students and teacher, home pressures, etc.

Academic Response Patterns

On the academic side, the teacher should generally respond in a positive way to correct responses [(*1*), (*2*)] and in a corrective way to incorrect responses (*4*). The desirable ratio of enthusiastic positives to unenthusiastic positives [(*1*) vs. (*2*)] varies greatly. Low functioning students or very young children require more enthusiastics, but all students will benefit from some amount of enthusiasm. Difficult responses call for more enthusiastic teacher responses than do easy or review responses. Too much enthusiasm for higher functioning students or for easy responses can make the teacher appear insincere or foolish.

All other categories under academic are to be avoided as errors, with three exceptions:

1. When the lesson is largely *review* in nature, many correct academic responses can be ignored (*6*). In effect, the schedule of reinforcement can be thinned. The students will know they were correct by implication. However, the lengthy sequences of correct responses should still receive approval [positive to correct, (*1*) or (*2*)] intermittently.

Supervisor __Piper__ — Teacher __Ms. Smith__ — Date __4/4__

Activity __Math instruction and work on sample problems – Class of 22 third graders, all participating, but with a group of 4 working with an aide.__

Time __10__ : __6__ to __10__ : __30__

Student Response to an Academic Task

Positive

(1)
```
II
TTHL II
TH
```
Really good thinking
Excellent, gives a star
Terrific

(2)
```
THT THT III
THT THT
THT II
```
good
OK
repeats answer & nods

(3)

Pupil Response Correct · Incor.

Corrective

(4)
```
THT THT THT
THT THT
```
Incor.

close, but not quite
gives explanation to
help correct error

Ignoring

(5)
Incor.

(6)
```
THT IIII
```
Correct

Ignores some answers
during brief review
drill

Negative

(7)
Incor. · Correct

(8)

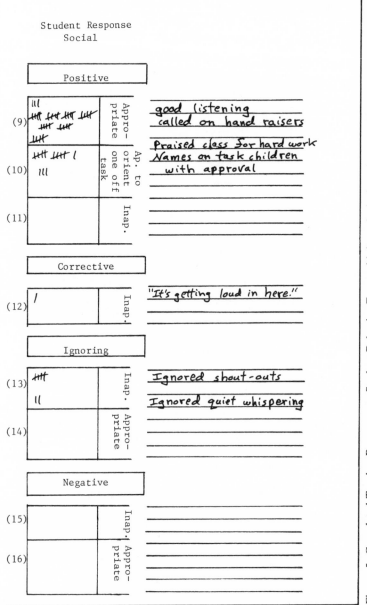

Student Response
Social

Positive

(9) ⦀ ⦀⦀⦀ ⦀⦀⦀ ⦀⦀⦀ ⦀⦀⦀ ⦀⦀⦀ ⦀⦀⦀ ⦀⦀⦀ | Appro-priate | *good listening* / *called on hand raisers*

(10) ⦀⦀⦀ ⦀⦀⦀ ⦀ / ⦀⦀⦀ | Ap. to orient one off task | *Praised class for hard work* / *Names on task children* / *with approval*

(11) | Inap.

Corrective

(12) ⦀ | Inap. | *"It's getting loud in here."*

Ignoring

(13) ⦀⦀⦀⦀ / ⦀⦀ | Inap. | *Ignored shout-outs* / *Ignored quiet whispering*

(14) | Appro-priate

Negative

(15) | Inap.

(16) | Appro-priate

Figure 5. Completed Teacher Response to Student Behavior Form with hypothetical entries. A well trained teacher.

51

Supervisor _Piper_   Teacher _Ms. Smith_   Date _11/1_

Activity _Math instruction and work on sample problems - class of 22 third graders, all participating, but with a group of 4 working with an aide._

Time _10_ : _10_ to _10_ : _30_

Student Response to an Academic Task

Positive		
(1)	‖‖‖ ‖‖ ‖‖ ‖‖‖‖‖‖	Correct — Pupil Response
(2)	‖‖‖‖‖ ‖ ‖‖‖‖‖ ‖‖‖‖‖ ‖‖	
(3)		Incor.

Excellent!
Pat on shoulder
Very good !
good
OK, right

Corrective		
(4)	‖‖‖‖‖ ‖‖‖‖‖ ‖‖‖‖‖ ‖‖‖	Incor.

provides added information
Try again

Ignoring		
(5)		Incor.
(6)	‖‖‖‖‖ ‖	Correct

moved on to next child
without comment

Negative		
(7)		Incor.
(8)		Correct

Figure 6. Completed Teacher Response to Student Behavior Form with hypothetical entries. A partially trained teacher.

Student Response
Social

Positive

(9) | / |
| /// |
| ЖЖ ЖЖ ЖЖ ЖЖ | Appro-priate

Thanked class for attention

calls on children raising hands

(10) | / | Ap. to orient one off task

"Is everyone where they're supposed to be like Mary + John?"

(11) | /// | Inap.

called on children shouting out answers

Corrective

(12) | //// |
| ЖЖ // | Inap.

Go back to your seat

We need less talking!

Ignoring

(13) | ЖЖ //// | Inap.

Ignored shout-outs

(14) | / → | Appro-priate

Ignored many children working + attending

Negative

(15) | / | Inap.

removed potatoe chips

(16) | / | Appro-priate

moved child's desk to corner

53

Supervisor *Piper* Teacher *Ms. Smith* Date *11/1*

Activity *Math instruction and work on sample problems – Class of 22 third*
graders, all participating, but with a group of 4 working with an aide.

Time *10 : 10* to *10 : 30*

Student Response to an Academic Task

Positive		
(1)	I	Pupil Response Correct
(2)	HTT / HTT HTT	
(3)		Incor.

Good – smile

right

repeats answer + nods

Corrective		
(4)	HTT III	Incor.

You're not thinking.
Try again

Ignoring		
(5)	II	Incor.
(6)	HTT HTT HTT II	Correct

Ignored error on blackboard
Ignored error in recitation

Moves on to next
question without comment

Negative		
(7)	HTT HTT	Incor. Correct
(8)		

No. Can someone else
do it?

54

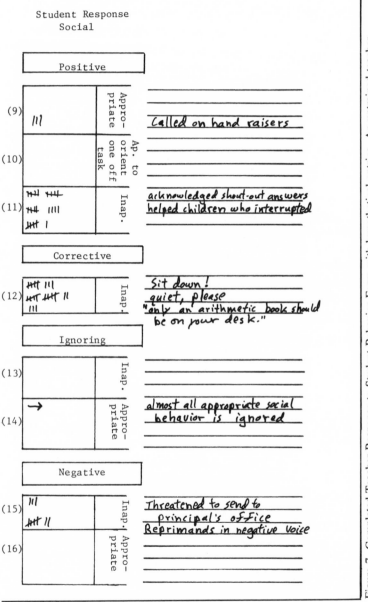

Student Response
Social

Positive

(9) ||| | Appro-priate | Called on hand raisers

(10) | Ap. to orient one off task |

(11) ₩₩ ₩₩ ₩₩ |||| ₩₩ | | Inap. | acknowledged shout-out answers helped children who interrupted

Corrective

(12) ₩₩ ||| ₩₩ ₩₩ || ||| | Inap. | Sit down! quiet, please "only an arithmetic book should be on your desk."

Ignoring

(13) | Inap. |

(14) → | Appro-priate | almost all appropriate social behavior is ignored

Negative

(15) ||| ₩₩ || | Inap. Appro-priate | Threatened to send to principal's office Reprimands in negative voice

(16) |

Figure 7. Completed Teacher Response to Student Behavior Form with hypothetical entries. An untrained teacher.

55

2. When an incorrect response is *perseverative* and the child has already proven to be insensitive to correctives, a negative to the incorrect *(7)* may be appropriate. Each negative should be counterbalanced by many positives.
3. When working with a very difficult task, very young children, or very low functioning students, the teacher may accept a less than correct response as correct in that it is the best the student has done (as in a *shaping procedure*). The teacher's apparent positive response to an incorrect *(3)* is in actuality a positive response to the best the student has done or can do.

The remaining categories are errors because they directly mislead students to accept a falsehood. Being positive to an incorrect is telling students that they're right when they're wrong. Similarly, being negative to a correct is telling students they're wrong when they're right. Ignoring an incorrect implies that the response was correct when it was not.

Social Response Patterns
The ideal pattern for social responses is somewhat different. Social responses differ from academic responses in that they are on-going. With few exceptions and in nearly all classes, the number of on-going appropriate social behaviors is greater than the number of inappropriate social behaviors at any given moment. Partly for this reason and because many inappropriate social behaviors are by their very nature attention getting, most teachers attend primarily, or exclusively, to inappropriate social behaviors. Appropriate social behavior is often taken for granted and consequently ignored. Without training, at least 9 of every 10 teachers display a pattern of attending almost exclusively to inappropriates when attending to social behavior. Yet the reverse is a far more desirable pattern.

In attending more often to appropriate behavior, the teacher is able to be predominately positive without making errors. By contrast, negative attention to inappropriate behavior will be more effective. Attention-seeking students will discover that they gain more attention by remaining on-task rather than off-task. The positive atmosphere of the class can be maintained. The teacher will appear to be a responsive, appreciative, positive manager. *Therefore, the most important single factor in responding to social behaviors has to do with whether the teacher responds more often to appropriate or to inappropriate behaviors.*

The teacher who responds to appropriate social behaviors in a negative way is, fortunately, rare. When a teacher learns to attend to appropriate behaviors, the teacher is almost always also learning to be positive. Training is conceptually easy, but the transition seems to be very difficult for many individuals. The predisposition to notice only inappropriates is often strong enough to require frequent feedback. The ideal pattern to be approximated from feedback is a frequency of positives to appropriates or to appropriate models [*(9), (10)*] that clearly exceeds the frequency of attention to all inappropriates combined [*(11), (12), (15)*]. When attention to inappropriates becomes necessary, as in the case of extremely disruptive or destructive behaviors, the attention should be negative *(15)*. Correctives *(12)*, reminding children of what they should be doing, should be infrequent. By attending to an appropriate model, the second category *(10)*, students can be reminded to get back to task without the possible reward of attention for being off-task.

Scoring in the ignoring categories is difficult for social behavior. If a student is in-seat and on-task for several minutes, how often has that appropriate behavior been ignored? Similarly, if a student is daydreaming instead, has the child been ignored once or a hundred times? All students in the class are exhibiting some sort of social behavior at all times, either on-task or off-task. Social behaviors vary enormously in duration and often have vague beginnings and endings. For these reasons, reliability is difficult or impossible to achieve in scoring the social ignoring categories [*(13), (14)*]. The categories, generally, are most useful when a particular social behavior of concern has been identified beforehand, either by the teacher or the supervisor. When it is hypothesized that an inappropriate behavior is performed for attention, and is not particularly dangerous, the teacher may be best advised to consistently ignore it *(13)* and attend to more desirable, incompatible behaviors [*(9)* or *(10)*]. Similarly, appropriate social behavior that occurs at very low rates, such as participation from a withdrawn child, should not be ignored *(14)*. *In summary, the ideal response pattern to social behaviors is one of high frequencies of positive attention to appropriate behavior [(9), (10)] and negative attention to disruptive or destructive behaviors (15) with the former occurring much more often than the latter.*

ADDITIONAL IMPLICATIONS
TO BE DRAWN FROM THE FORM

Rate of Interaction

In addition to the pattern of interaction, recording interaction in this way also indicates rate of interaction. For a given teacher, the pattern of interaction tends to be relatively constant, but rate is subject to wide variation. The nature of the on-going lesson, for example, is likely to profoundly affect rate. However, after many observations, a supervisor will be able to judge whether a teacher tends to display a high or a low overall rate. Although the quality of interaction is certainly the most potent variable in rapport, unusual rates of interaction may suggest special strengths or weaknesses. Unusually low rates might be a function of a teacher who lectures to excess, or fails to respond to student's behavior. It may also suggest that the students avoid interacting with the teacher because doing so proves to be unproductive or aversive. It is also possible that low rates are a function of the teacher having trained the students to be self-directed or to rely upon each other to an unusual degree.

High rates are generally a positive sign, but may indicate too much direction from the teacher as well. Adjectives such as "enthusiastic," "energetic," and "dynamic" tend to be associated with high rates of interaction. Whether or not an unusual rate seems to be an asset to the teacher, or a deficit, should be evident to the supervisor. The record will substantiate the supervisor's impressions regarding strengths or weaknesses. Although rate is a very gross measure, the teacher who has a difficulty related to rate may find feedback on this variable exceedingly helpful.

Feedback in Curriculum Planning

The academic side of the form may also provide information regarding the lesson taught, as well as a pattern of interaction. If, in a particular observation, the number of correctives is very high relative to the number of positives to corrects, the lesson was probably too difficult. The teacher may need to do more to assess current levels of functioning. In the opposite case, many positives to corrects and no correctives, the lesson would seem to be either too easy or for review purposes only. Should a tendency toward either extreme repeat itself over many observations, the supervisor should consult with the teacher regarding curriculum planning.

SUGGESTIONS FOR
PROVIDING FEEDBACK TO THE TEACHER

The form is sufficiently complex to account for nearly every response a teacher may make to pupils while remaining sufficiently simple to be clearly understood. Although the form becomes increasingly simple to the observer with use, it is important to remember how complex it probably appeared initially. The complexity can be frightening. To make the initial observations more difficult, very few teachers are accustomed to having their responses categorized and recorded. The observer must prepare the teacher for the observation. The form must be sufficiently understood and the teacher sufficiently comfortable before the benefits of feedback can be realized.

In-Service Presentation of Form to Teachers

The most efficient procedure is likely to be some sort of in-service presentation wherein the supervisor explains the form and its purpose. Beware of the danger of only partial understanding. Also, be prepared to honestly answer all questions related to teacher evaluations. Formal use of the form in evaluation is best postponed until it is well understood and is no longer threatening to the teachers.

A 15-minute video tape of a lesson can prove very helpful. Record a teacher's responses on a form on an overhead projector. The teacher who volunteers to be taped for this purpose will probably perform well. The strengths of the teacher will be perceived by the audience. Participants will feel assured when these strengths are recorded and interpreted for them at the end of the tape. As soon as possible after the presentation, each participant should be observed and feedback provided. Initial observations will serve to develop the recording skills of the observer as well as to familiarize the teacher. When 142 teachers in suburban Philadelphia were asked to comment on the form after field testing, only 4 objected to its use. Ninety-six made clearly favorable comments. The benefits of useful feedback quickly outweigh the potential threats implied by objective recording for the great majority of teachers.

Feedback for support and/or improvement should be the primary purpose of observing. Never record an observation without providing face-to-face feedback. When providing feedback, begin with entries that reflect a strength or asset. Where there are deficits or errors, explain the categories carefully and ask the teacher to interpret the recording. After teachers are sufficiently informed regarding the form, most can be expected to interpret and explain the results to the supervisor. Notes should be taken whenever an entry is recorded that seems to be an error, so that the specific instance can be recalled. Teachers will either clarify apparent errors or gain maximally from errors when an abstract tally mark can be recalled as a real event during the observation. Since the supervisor as well as the teacher should be positive, notes should also be made regarding especially good, creative, or interesting responses.

Chapter 3
Observing Individualized Instruction

RATIONALE FOR INDIVIDUALIZED INSTRUCTION

The arguments against group instruction are well known by educators. Faster students in the group are held back. Slower students, finding academic tasks impossible because of missing curriculum, (*i.e.,* curriculum already taught but not yet learned), may be left behind. Many groups progress at the rate of the slowest member.

Individualization of instruction is especially important in the tool subjects related to reading and arithmetic, or any curriculum in which there is a hierarchy of skills with elementary levels of success required before progressing to higher levels. Therefore, teachers have a far greater responsibility to individualize in certain curricular areas. Special education teachers, remedial reading teachers, or any other teachers with an unusually small class enrollment have more responsibility to individualize.

There are degrees of individualization. The teacher of 35 children is certainly doing an admirable job to have 3 reading groups and 3 math groups, even though group membership may exceed 12. The learning disabilities teacher with only 10 students should probably have approximately 10 reading groups most of the time, each child progressing at his own rate. Teaching is difficult and individualizing the process multiplies the difficulties. As the school year progresses, the teacher can benefit greatly by receiving support and appreciation from the supervisor for efforts to individualize.

COLLECTING QUANTITATIVE INFORMATION REGARDING INDIVIDUALIZED INSTRUCTION

The first part of this chapter is addressed to the problem of determining whether individualization is taking place, the second to the quality of the individualization. In the first part, a means is given of observing individualization directly, as objectively as possible, without regard for the quality of the individualization. This is done through the Individualization Form (Figure 8), which is filled out by the supervisor. The quality of individualization, addressed in the second part, is determined through two forms which are filled out by the teacher, the Assessment Form (Figures 9 through 12) and the On-Going Assessment Report Form (Figures 13 through 16).

INDIVIDUALIZATION FORM

The Individualization Form (Figure 8, pages 64, 65) is most conveniently printed on the opposite side of the Teacher Response to Student Behavior (or rapport) Form, which appears in Figures 4–7. These two forms are the only two used during the observation itself and therefore require the supervisor to manipulate only one paper for data collection purposes. It must be remembered that quality of individualization is not reflected in the items on the form. To observe quality objectively in the relatively brief time that most supervisors have to observe is impossible, but to observe variables likely to be associated with individualization is relatively simple.

The most obvious variable is the number of reading or math (or whatever the teacher claims to individualize) groups. The number of groups for such subjects is common knowledge in any classroom. The supervisor would most probably ask the teacher for the information, but aides and the children themselves will also know. The larger the number of groups per individualized subject, the more probable it is that individualization is actually taking place.

A highly similar, and directly observable, variable is the number of students the teacher teaches at one time. Suppose the teacher has 12 students in a special education class and addresses all 12 as a group for an entire 20 minutes. By implication, there is little individualization. On the other hand, the teacher might work with 3 children, then 1, then on to a group of 4, then 2, and so on. The movement within the class implies a great deal of individualization. Should the teacher have an aide, the same observation might be made of the aide.

Highly related to the variables already described is the number of different academic tasks on-going at particular moments in time. Again, as the number of different tasks approaches the number of children in the classroom, individualization would seem increasingly probable. If all children are doing the same task, individualization is, at that time, not taking place.

Especially in larger classrooms, individualization is very difficult unless children are prepared to self-initiate tasks. When enrollment surpasses 10 or 15, as in most classrooms, the teacher cannot evaluate each child's task completion before allowing the child to go on to the next task. Instead, the child must self-initiate the next task. Examples of classroom organizations that encourage self-initiation are classrooms that extensively utilize commercially prepared materials in which the child evaluates his own work, or classes where the teacher provides each child with a folder containing a sizable number of tasks. There are a multitude of organizational possibilities, but some form of self-initiation is necessary in all. The supervisor who observes many children self-initiating tasks is observing a class where individualization is possible, even when enrollment figures are high.

Individualization

(1) Number of different academic tasks on-going

time   number of tasks

_____   _____
_____   _____
_____   _____

(2) Number of groups in each major subject area

subject   groups

_____   _____
_____   _____
_____   _____
_____   _____

(3) Number of students that teacher is presenting material to

#: _____   : _____

(4) Number of students teacher aide is presenting material to

#_____ :_____

_____ :_____

(5) Number of "academic" tasks initiated without a directive from a teacher immediately preceding the tasks.

_____

_____

_____

Figure 8. Individualization Form.

65

Five items are included on the form. All are designed to be relatively easy to complete. The experienced supervisor can learn to take advantage of pauses in teacher-student interaction to complete items on the Individualization Form simultaneously with the Teacher Response to Student Behavior Form (Figures 4–7).

Number of Tasks Variable

The first item *(1)* accounts for the number of different tasks on-going within certain time samples. Space is provided for three samples or observations. All three need not be utilized or the form easily may be expanded to provide space for more than three. When time is available, and at intervals widely spaced during the observation, the supervisor records the time of day at the left and the number of tasks at the right. Generally, a record made at the beginning, midway, and end of the observation should be adequate. The supervisor may have to stand and/or move about the room in order to ascertain what the students are doing.

Number of Groups Variable

Item *(2)* is the easiest to record because, as already mentioned, the supervisor can ask nearly anyone in the classroom. In this sense, the item is not a direct observation of behavior, but a recording of information probably provided by the teacher. The item asks for the number of groups there are in each curricular area that the teacher claims to individualize to some extent. Space is provided for listing five subjects and can be expanded, should the need present itself. The supervisor lists the subjects on the left, and the number of groups on the right. Higher numbers of subjects and higher numbers of groups suggest greater individualization.

Number of Students to Whom
Material Is Presented Variables

Items *(3)* and *(4)* are identical except that in *(3)*, the teacher is observed and in *(4)*, the aide is observed. If there is no aide, the supervisor indicates that item *(4)* is not applicable. The item records the number of children the teacher interacts with at given moments in time over a sample of time, at least 15 minutes. The smaller the number of children relative to the class size as a whole, and the more frequently the teacher moves from one subgroup or individual, to another, the greater the probability of individualization. The top line is a time line. The initial time of observation is recorded to the far left, the final time of observation to the far right. Immediately below the time, the supervisor records the number of children receiving direct instruction at that moment.

Time Entries

Entries of time, usually only the minutes of the hour, are recorded along the time line whenever the teacher's instructional group or individual addressed changes. With each time entry, the number of children in the new group is entered directly below. Except in classrooms where the teacher both individualizes a great deal and moves frequently, the observational task is not as time consuming as it might appear. Other observations can be made simultaneously.

Number of Self-Initiated Tasks Variable

The last item *(5)* refers to the number of tasks the supervisor can observe that are self-initiated by the children. If the self-initiation involves gross body movements so that the frequency within a sample of time is easily observable, the first two (shorter) lines are used. A slash mark (/) is made for each occurrence and a rate can be calculated by dividing the number of slashes by the number of minutes observed. Higher rates make individualization more possible, especially in larger classes.

The frequency of self-initiated tasks is not always easy to observe as in the larger class where children are working at their seats from folders containing multiple tasks. To notice every time a child begins a new worksheet would require all of the supervisor's attention and might call for moving about the room to the distraction of everyone. In this case, the supervisor may make more casual observations and record the observation in sentence form on the last two lines of the form.

COLLECTING QUALITATIVE INFORMATION REGARDING INDIVIDUALIZED INSTRUCTION

In the preceding section, observational items were listed that had to do with ascertaining, in an objective manner, whether or not the teacher was individualizing instruction. The items are independent of quality of individualization. In this section of the chapter, the question of quality will be addressed.

Certain subjects, especially reading, math, and language skills, must progress in a sequential manner. Elementary skills are mastered before more advanced skills because skills are built one upon another. Although there may be alternatives in the skill sequences, the necessity of mastering initial skills before later skills remains. The nature of these curricular areas places a greater responsibility upon the teacher to individualize. That is, the teacher must be aware of the particular skill sequence used in the class, school, or system; then the teacher must attempt to identify each student's position in that skill sequence; finally, the teacher must present lessons designed for each student's current level of functioning relative to the skill seqeunce.

Assessment Form

The supervisor is likely to supervise at least 10 teachers, and in some instances 100 or more. The teachers may be scattered over many schools. It is unrealistic, in almost all cases, to expect the supervisor to know whether or not the work given a particular student is appropriate for that student. The supervisor must have information from the teacher regarding the program or skill sequence, and each child's current level of functioning. The teacher must, then, formalize some sort of assessment procedure and must have programatic information at hand in order for the supervisor to evaluate the quality of individualization.

The forms already discussed are filled out by the supervisor during observations. The forms to be presented here are filled out by the teacher before the supervisor arrives.

The Assessment Form (Figure 9, pages 70, 71; Figures 10–12, pages 72–77) is filled out for each student in each subject in which the teacher claims to individualize. In regular classes, the form may be filled out at the beginning of the school year and again at the end. In specialized classes such as a resource room, a special education class, or the remedial reading teacher's class, the form may be filled in quarterly, or even monthly. One county-wide special education system has adapted the assessment form to serve as a report card, submitted to the parents four times during the school year. The teacher should note that with the proper use of this form in those subject areas individualized the forms may eliminate or modify:

1. Daily lesson plan books
2. Periodic scheduled reports (daily logs, monthly reports)
3. Separate lesson plans and evaluation reports
4. Substitute teacher instructions
5. Confusion regarding exact behaviors in the process of being changed/modified
6. Use of the traditional report card

Description of Entries The upper left-hand quartile of space is for a brief summary of observations of assessment. These may be test scores, summaries of inventories, informal observations, or whatever the teacher uses to ascertain those skills already mastered in the subject area at hand. In the lower left-hand quartile, the teacher indicates skills for which the child has the greatest current need. The teacher makes a brief assessment and from it indicates where instructional efforts will be concentrated first. The same kinds of entries are made on the right-hand side, after enough time has passed to require an update. If the right-hand side is filled out at the end of the year, it may be of most use to the teacher who receives the child the next year. The new teacher would have at hand the previous teacher's summary of

```

                                                      Assessment

                Student_____

                Curriculum Area
                _____

                             September or
                _____

                Most Advanced Objectives Met









                _____

                Long Range Goals










```

Figure 9. Assessment Form.

Form

    Teacher_____.

    School Year_____

                      June or

Most Advanced Objectives Met

Long Range Goals

Assessment

Student **Bobbie**

Curriculum Area
Locomotion

September or

Most Advanced Objectives Met

1. Bobbie spends most of his time lying on the floor.
2. He can pull himself with his arms but doesn't use his legs.
3. His arm muscles are well developed and strong.
4. There is no obvious reason why he cannot learn to use his legs.
5. He lacks motivation and is used to having things done for him at home.
6. He expects to have things done for him at school.

Long Range Goals

1. Strengthen legs, trunk and balance with use of standing table - increase time to about ½ hour/day.
2. Learn to use rollator walker (with help of strap and someone to pull him) to get to PT (20 feet) in less than 3 minutes.
3. Use wheelchair without help.
4. Transfer self from floor to chair without help.
5. Possibly learn to walk with crutches (several years).

Figure 10. Completed Assessment Form with hypothetical entries.

Form

Teacher___*Physically Handicapped*___

School Year___*'78- '79*___

June or

Most Advanced Objectives Met

Long Range Goals

Assessment

Student __Roger__

Curriculum Area

__Reading__

September or
_____

Most Advanced Objectives Met
1. 90% accuracy on vocabulary (reading orally from p.97 of <u>Something New</u> Level 3).
2. 95% accuracy naming beginning consonants (from work sheet level K-2).
3. 10% accuracy supplying missing short vowels (p.53 workbook <u>Something New</u>).
4. 50% accuracy spelling words (p. 10 <u>Spelling for You</u> Level 1).
5. 10% accuracy repeating four-letter nonsense words after 10 sec. reviewing each.

Long Range Goals
1. Begin Level 2-2 of <u>Harper & Row</u> Reading Series
   a. 95% accuracy on vocabulary recognition.
   b. concentrate on vowels (90% accuracy).
2. Begin Level Primer <u>Spelling for You</u>
   a. 85% accuracy spelling
   b. 100% accuracy on applying seven basic rules outlined in book for spelling regular words.
3. Begin Level 3 <u>Sullivan Programmed</u> Reading concentrating on phonic skills involved in spelling words (95% accuracy spelling words introduced).
4. Outline program to improve visual memory.

Figure 11. Completed Assessment Form with hypothetical entries.

Form

Teacher____*Elem. LD*____

School Year____*'78 - '79*____

June or
_____

Most Advanced Objectives Met

Long Range Goals

Student ___Roscoe_____

Curriculum Area
_____Reading_____

September or
_____

Most Advanced Objectives Met

9/9/74 - Silvaroli - Classroom Reading Inventory Form A
    Independent - Grade 2
    Instructional - Grade 3
    Frustrational - Grade 4
    Hearing Capacity - Grade 3
9/10/74 - Palo Alto Reading Program
    Informal Testing - Books 17 + 18
    Reading from books and success observed

Long Range Goals

Good phonetic analysis skills but needs work
  in comprehension.

Work on main ideas and drawing conclusions
  from material read.

Figure 12. Completed Assessment Form with hypothetical entries.

Form

Teacher_____ *Ms. Rantz* _____

School Year_____

June or

Most Advanced Objectives Met

Long Range Goals

On-Going Assessment

Student _____

Subject _____

Learning Objective   Date
(Instructional Goals)   Begun

Figure 13. On-Going Assessment Report Form.

Report Form

Cooperating Teacher _____

Trainee _____

Date
Mastered   Materials

Student _Roscoe_

Subject _Reading_

Learning Objective (Instructional Goals)	Date Begun
Given 10 sentences, the student will be able to underline the topic word in that sentence with 100% accuracy.	9/10/78
Given a paragraph, the student will be able to underline the first sentence and the last sentence in the paragraph with 100% accuracy.	9/11/78
Given a picture, the student will be able to say three things that he thinks are happening in the picture.	9/12/78
Given a series of pictures, the student will be able to place these pictures in order to make a good story as judged by teacher.	9/13/78
Given a paragraph, the student will be able to answer three questions about the content of that paragraph with 100% accuracy.	9/10/78

Figure 14. Completed On-Going Assessment Report Form with hypothetical entries.

Report Form

Cooperating Teacher _Ms. Rantz_

Trainee _____

Date Mastered	Materials
9/13/78	- Ditto sheets - teacher made. No problem in this activity.
9/11/78	- Ditto sheets - teacher made. Objective set too low - child mastered quickly with no difficulty.
9/12/78	- DLM Posters. Enjoyed this activity
9/18/78	- DLM Picture Cards. Asked to do more of this activity. Opportunity to tell reading group of the stories.
9/26/78	- Specific Skills Series Level A and Level B "Getting the Main Idea" "Drawing Conclusions" "Getting the Facts" - Retest on Silvaroli - 9/27/78 Independent - Grade 2 Instructional - Grade 3 Frustrational - Grade 4 Hearing Capacity - Grade 6 Comprehension improved - on grade with word recognition.

Student   Bobbie

Subject   Locomotion

Learning Objective (Instructional Goals)	Date Begun

1. Given a standing table, a simple manipulative hand task, *five* minutes and placed in a standing position,
    Bobbie will stand without slumping
    (five consecutive days)
	9/20/78

2. Given a wheel chair appropriate for him, the direction, "Pull yourself into your chair" and *ten* minutes, Bobbie will pull himself from the floor to his chair (five consecutive days)	9/20/78

3. Given *ten* minutes, the direction, "Meet you at lunch," and a seated position in his wheel chair,
    Bobbie will wheel himself the twenty feet to the cafeteria to eat lunch
    (five consecutive days)
	10/3/78

4. Given a rollator, *one* minute, and placed in position, Bobbie will stand in the rollator without slumping (five consecutive days)	10/8/78
5. Given a standing table, *ten* minutes, and placed in position, Same as Objective 1	10/8/78
6. Given a wheel chair, *five* minutes, the direction, "Meet you at lunch." Same as Objective 2	10/20/78

Figure 15. Completed On-Going Assessment Report Form with hypothetical entries.

Report Form

Cooperating Teacher <u>Physically Handicapped</u>

Trainee _____

Date Mastered	Materials
	Standing table, parquet blocks
10/8/78	
10/1/78	
10/20/78	Bobbie needs the incentive of getting lunch. He has to wait until someone "has time" to get his lunch. The wait is purposely 5 or 10 minutes as Bobbie is capable of getting there easily in time allotted.

On-Going Assessment

Student   Roger

Subject   Reading

Learning Objective (Instructional Goals)	Date Begun
1. Given the ten new vocabulary words (on Flash cards) from pages 50-90 of his reader and five seconds each, Roger will name the words correctly with 100% accuracy	11/5/78
2. Given a worksheet of twenty pictures of one syllable words containing short vowels and ten minutes, Roger will correctly fill in the missing vowel with 100% accuracy	11/7/78
3. Given the ten new vocabulary words from pages 90-120 Same as Objective 1	11/12/78

Figure 16. Completed On-Going Assessment Report Form with hypothetical entries.

Report Form

Cooperating Teacher <u>Elem. L. D.</u>

Trainee <u> </u>

Date Mastered	Materials
11/12/78	Vocabulary list on page 7 of T. Ed., flashcards, daily drill with aide Something <u>New</u> phonics workbook <u>Phonics We Use D</u> - drill pages on short vowels <u>Sullivan Programmed Reader</u> - <u>Vowel Lotto</u> played bi-weekly with aide

each student's level of functioning at the end of the preceding year, and recommendations regarding what was needed most at that time. Checklists, when very carefully developed, may serve the same purpose.

Information Provided by Assessment Form To the supervisor, the assessment form provides valuable information regarding:

1. The teacher's assessment procedures
2. The degree to which current instructional placements are appropriate
3. The degree to which instructional plans are coordinated with need

Without such knowledge, the supervisor is placed in an extremely difficult position if the teacher wishes help or guidance from the supervisor in this respect.

On-Going Assessment Report Form

Overall assessments can be very time consuming. Even in the smaller special classes, they are not likely to be done more than four or six times per school year. The teacher needs time to teach as well as to assess. The need to assess is greatly reduced if the teacher identifies long and short range goals based upon the original assessment. Special education teachers are required to identify goals in almost all systems. The regular classroom teacher can similarly identify goals often provided by the reading or math series in use in the classroom.

The On-Going Assessment Report Form shown in Figure 13 (pages 78, 79), with sample forms in Figures 14–16 (pages 80–85), is designed to reduce the need for frequent, more generic assessments. The teacher identifies the first goal most appropriate for a child in an individualized subject. When that goal is reached, the curriculum sequence itself provides succeeding goals. These in turn are recorded. After months pass, the teacher may reassess all areas in order to assure a uniform progression across subject areas.

When a supervisor observes instruction in a room where the teacher can provide completed assessment reports as well as on-going assessment reports, the supervisor cannot only observe the individualization, he can evaluate the quality as well. The teacher provides all the information the supervisor will need to help the teacher improve instruction or to give the teacher alternatives in the instructional effort:

1. The assessment procedure from which the initial instructional goal was identified is known
2. The current goal for each student is known
3. The rate at which the student meets goals is known
4. The materials that the teacher is using are known

Instructional goals on the On-Going Assessment Report Form may be written as complete instructional objectives (Mager, 1962),[1] or may be abbreviated, depending on the detail required by the supervisor in order to intelligently fulfill the supervisory role. Each goal is listed under the last goal met. Additional forms are attached to the first On-Going Assessment Report Form as the need for more space arises.

---

[1] A complete system of writing these behavioral objectives is detailed in the following chapter.

Chapter 4

Writing Behavioral Objectives

WHAT ARE BEHAVIORAL OBJECTIVES?

The term "behavioral objective" is synonymous with that of performance objective and may be considered the same as a learning objective or learning goal. A behavioral or performance objective is a description of a specific learning task including some measure which indicates the accomplishment of that task. Objectives must be based on the assessment of student needs and strengths and are determined as a result of the identification of areas of teaching concentration necessary for the student.

ADVANTAGES OF USING BEHAVIORAL OBJECTIVES

After the assessment and after determining the educational diagnosis, the actual writing of objectives is the third in the sequence of activities used to ensure that individual attention is given to each student for each subject. Teachers may resist writing objectives in an effort to avoid additional paperwork. However, the advantages to using behavioral objectives are many. Given the use of objectives, teachers will be able to:

1. State criteria for evaluating the learner's performance
2. Arrange sequences of courses or units of instruction
3. Plan with their students a sequence of courses or units of instruction
4. Tell other teachers what they teach
5. Design instructional experiences and evaluate the effectiveness of such experiences according to whether the goals are achieved
6. Determine the students' capabilities at any given time during the instructional program
7. Report to parents the students' current programs in terms that describe what the students are doing rather than in terms that compare one student to another in relationship to an achievement level expectation
8. State their specific instructional goals to their immediate supervisors
9. Determine the adequacy of the instructional program and make changes accordingly
10. Coordinate curriculum materials and instructional goals in a more direct relationship
11. Document individualization
12. Better meet the requirements of Public Law 94-142 which requires special education teachers to establish both long term and short term goals

Behavioral objectives may also be of help to students. The objectives:

1. Identify short term goals for the student, based on his/her current level of functioning, that are relatively easy to attain (*i.e.*, they will give the student something for which to aim)
2. Help the student to understand the purpose for instructional activities
3. Assure success experiences when goals are achieved

4. Assure feedback regarding goal approximations
5. Help the student to associate short term goals with broader long term goals

COMPONENTS OF BEHAVIORAL OBJECTIVES

A behavioral objective consists of three basic components. It must:

1. Clearly specify an observable behavior which is to be learned
2. Describe the conditions under which the behavior is to be learned
3. Indicate a measure of performance which gives evidence of the accomplishment of the objective—*i.e.*, show that the learner has learned what he/she was supposed to have learned

SAMPLE OBJECTIVES

In order to examine this more completely, observe some sample objectives and note the essential elements.

Given a blue, a yellow and a red block and the instruction, "Hand me the red block," the student will be able to hand to the teacher the red block in six out of six trials.

Given the numerals, 1 through 6, each printed on a separate card and exposed to the student one at a time with the question, "What number is this?," the student will identify each of the numerals exposed on four out of five trials for each numeral.

Given a zipper-front coat and the instruction, "Put this coat on," the student will be able to put his coat on without assistance on four out of four trials on 2 successive days.

Supplying Measurable Components in Behavioral Objectives

Each of the above objectives contains all three basic components. The first of these is that the behavior be clearly specified and observable. For example, to understand or to really understand are not observable behaviors. In order that a behavior be

specified, it must indicate exactly what is to take place. In order
for a behavior to be observable, it must be one which can be seen
or measured. Look at the measurable, observable components of
the objectives below:

The student will be able to hand to the teacher the red block.

The student will identify each of the numerals exposed.

The student will be able to put his coat on without assistance.

The underscored portion indicates the measurable component of
each objective. Obviously, a child can either hand to you or not
hand to you a block, or will be able to either identify or not
identify numerals 1 through 6. These behaviors are easily
measurable and identifiable.

Measurable Terms Compare, then, such measurable terms
as list, identify, describe, choose, with terms commonly seen in
objectives such as know, understand, appreciate, and so on. One
can immediately ascertain what behavior is desired if one is to
list a number of items or to describe an event in one paragraph.
One would have a great deal of difficulty trying to ascertain the
desired behavior in understanding Poe's *Raven* or appreciating
a work of art. Desired behaviors are therefore stated in terms
which lend themselves to measurement. Some terms which are
easily measurable are:

list	place in order
describe	answer
count	classify
identify	demonstrate
write	recite
choose	

Conditions of the Objective One must examine the conditions under which these behaviors are to occur. Behavior does not
occur in a vacuum. It occurs in some sort of an experimental
context. The context provides meaning to the behavior that oc-

curs. For an example, examine one of the objectives already described.

The student will be able to identify each of the numerals exposed.

A specific behavior is desired; yet the behavior alone lacks specificity. The realm of numbers that could be used is infinite. Is he going to identify all possible numbers? How many numbers is he expected to identify? The answers to these questions are provided by the statement of the conditions under which the desired behavior is to occur.

Given the numerals 1 through 6 each printed on a separate card and exposed to the student one at a time with the question, "What number is this?," the student will be able to identify each of the numerals exposed.

The underscored portion in the above has two functions. It first establishes the context in which the specified behavior is to occur and also describes the stimulus for eliciting the desired behavior. Seen in behavioral terms, the conditions provide the antecedents or stimuli for the desired behavior, and the behavior indicates the response to these antecedents.

Form of the Objective A note may also be made about the form of the objectives at this point. Each one begins with "Given...." Although this beginning cannot be universally applied, beginning the objective statement with given immediately structures the conditions for the behavior and provides a logical flow from stimulus (*conditions*) to response (*desired behavior*). This allows for a less complicated flow for writing of objectives that is easier and less awkward than writing the objective in most other ways.

Measurement of Criteria for Performance Once the desired behavior and the conditions under which it is to occur are described, one needs a means to measure whether the behavior is occurring as desired. The measure of whether the behavior is occurring as desired is termed the *criteria for performance* or *criteria.* The criteria build into the objective the measurement which determines whether the desired behavior has or has not been achieved. By following the stated criteria, it is determined whether one should move on to another objective or whether one should continue working with the present objective. This example clarifies:

> Given the numerals 1 through 6, each printed on a separate card and exposed to the student one at a time with the question, "What number is this?," the student will identify each of the numerals exposed on four out of five trials for each numeral.

Determining Achievement Level of an Objective

In order to have any validity the objective is determined according to the assessment of the student's needs and on the basis of determining the areas for teaching concentration which are derived through the assessment. A rule of thumb for determining where to begin is to determine the area in a particular subject indicated through assessment as being the student's lowest level of functioning. For instance, a student may, on a math assessment, show that he can tell time to half-hour segments, recognize money values to a quarter, do additional problems for one-column and two-column addition, and do simple addition word problems. The student also may be unable to match numerals to the number of objects in a group to 20. In determining where to begin with this student, the lowest level of achievement is the matching of numerals to the number of objects in a group. It would be logical to write the first objective for extending the student's achievement in this area.

Determining Time Range of an Objective

When thinking of just how long range an objective should be, it is most pragmatic to develop objectives which the teacher expects the student to meet in about 2 weeks. In some cases, this is impractical. With some lower functioning students or young children, one may wish the desired behavior to be achieved to criteria in a few days. However, one would rarely want to begin on a new objective every day, nor should a student be working on the same objective for the whole year. In most situations, 1 to 2 weeks is the most desirable period for a student to be working on a particular objective until he/she achieves criteria.

RESOURCES FOR
ORGANIZING AND WRITING OBJECTIVES

Available Materials

Ideally, a teacher should establish learning objectives for his/her students and then use the materials needed to meet these objectives. This is not always possible. It is particularly difficult for new teachers who have not accumulated a working knowledge of curriculum steps or for teachers limited in the materials available to them. There are several avenues open to these teachers. They may:

1. Check the teacher's edition of the books used. These often have their own list of behavioral objectives. Although these may be much too broad for use, they can give a general idea of what to include in the objectives.
2. Check the inside covers of workbooks, both teachers' and pupils'. Often the publisher will list the specific skills covered and the pages on which these skills are presented.
3. Check to see whether texts include test materials. These can be incorporated easily into behavioral objectives.

Sample Objectives

Using these avenues, and a standard basal reader, a few behavioral objectives for a hypothetical child are presented.

Example 1   In the Harper and Row *Patterns in Design for Reading* (Hamp, O'Donnell, and Greenlaw, 1974) behavioral objective no. 1 reads:

> In order to demonstrate his ability to communicate orally the meaning conveyed by printed language, the student will read aloud material of an appropriate difficulty level with acceptable standard pronunciation and with reasonable fluency of expression.

Translated into an objective for the child, this might read:

> Given 10 consecutive sentences from her present reader, Carol will read the sentences:
> 1. With correct pronunciation
> 2. Without pausing to recognize vocabulary
> 3. Altering voice inflection appropriate to punctuation
> 4. For three consecutive reading periods.

Example 2 On the inside cover of the student's workbook of this same series is found the listing:

> Linguistic Skills
> Sound Symbol Relations
>   Vowels, short 14, 17, 24, 30, 53, 82, 89, 112

This information might be translated into the following objective:

> Given 30 pictures of objects whose names are one-syllable words containing a short vowel, Carol will correctly fill in the missing vowel in the printed word under the picture with 100% accuracy.

Both of these objectives may be too long range and can be broken down, but both will give the teacher a starting point upon which to draw for the child's ongoing assessment.

Example 3 Take advantage of such things as vocabulary lists. An appropriate objective might be:

> Given flash cards of the 10 new words introduced between pages 1 and 19 of her reader and 10 seconds each, Carol will name the words with 100% accuracy.

Take advantage of the teacher material provided by the publishers of texts. The time it takes to read this material may be more than worth it when it comes to organizing objectives.

Chapter 5
Feedback
to the Teacher

With any sort of studied observation, the teacher should be given feedback regarding that which was observed. Feedback may be brief or lengthy and complex. Without feedback, the teacher may feel intimidated by the supervisor, but of more importance, the observation will have served no constructive purpose regarding change in the teacher's behavior. Learning, or change in behavior, is unlikely without feedback.

COMPLETE AND FORMAL OBSERVATION

As an example of feedback, let us begin with the complete and formal observation. The complete observation will include observations of the teacher's rapport and classroom structure for individualization as well as review of assessment records and short and long range goals or behavioral objectives derived from assessment information. The supervisor will also consider the relationship between lesson(s) observed and objectives, as well as the teacher's system of record keeping regarding the criteria established for objectives. Additional variables may be formally observed as well. Other variables might include items unique to the particular classroom or those observations that the supervisor has historically recorded because of specifications of the school system or those that the supervisor feels to be of importance but that have not adequately been observed by the system presented here. The proposed system is not intended to eliminate more subjective observational information except where the information gathering is redundant. In that case, objectivity is preferred to subjectivity. Objective information is, by definition, more precise and less affected by the supervisor's personal values and can therefore be expected to have more power in affecting teacher behavior.

PURPOSES OF FORMAL OBSERVATION

The form for summarizing the complete observation has multiple purposes. These are:

1. To facilitate summarizing the whole observation
2. To record progress on objectives established for the teacher in the past and to record newly established objectives
3. To be useful to both supervisor and the teacher in helping the teacher establish his or her own objectives
4. To serve as the permanent record of the observation in the teacher's file

SUPERVISORY REPORT FORM

The Supervisory Report form (Figure 17, pages 100–103; Figure 18, pages 104–107) is an example that can be easily modified to reflect the concerns of the school district involved.

Section I

The first item *(I)* is an abbreviation of a particular district's traditional form with the elimination of items that will be reflected in other sections of the form. Notice that the items tend to be very easy to observe and record. Therefore, a very limited amount of space is provided for making comments on each item. The items are easily altered from system to system, but most will be included in any traditional system. A rating system, *e.g.,* from "very satisfactory" to "very unsatisfactory," is again avoided because of the implication that it is the supervisor's opinion, rather than fact, that is inherent on any rating system format. Comments, where necessary, should be kept as objective as possible. The brevity of space provided for these items is also a function of an effort to limit the form to one piece of paper, both sides used, so that permanent or long term files of observational records will not become too bulky or cumbersome.

Section II

The second section of the form *(II)* relates directly to information gathering on the Individualization Form (Figure 8), the Assessment Form (Figures 9–12), and the On-Going Assessment Report Form (Figures 13–16). The section has greater importance to special educators and remedial teachers or tutors. The section might be shortened for regular classroom teachers in favor of more space for later sections.

The three items listed under Section II of Figure 17 are reasonably self-explanatory. Assessment and appropriate selection of diagnostic inventories *(A)* provides space for comment regarding the assessment procedure(s) and records of assessment provided by the teacher. The information should be already available from the Assessment Form (Figures 9–12). The supervisor comments on the desirability of selections made for a particular purpose, may suggest others, or may express concern over missing or inadequate assessment information.

"Writing Behavioral Objectives" *(B)* provides space for comment on the teacher's ability to write behavioral objectives of any kind, and to select objectives that assessment information would suggest are most appropriate for a given child or group of children. It is also here that a reference can be made regarding the relationship(s) between recorded objectives and the lessons observed being taught.

Supervisory Report Form

Teacher Observed: _____   Time of Observation: __:__ to __:__

School and Class: _____   Date: _____

Number of Pupils: _____   Observer: _____

I. Classroom and School Variables
A. Physical (as far as the teacher can control)

Class Layout: _____

External Noise, Heat, Light, Ventilation _____
Cleanliness, Orderliness _____
Furniture appropriate and of right size _____
Materials, equipment, and resources (including supportive personnel)
    accessible and used _____
Safety precautions _____
Bulletin boards, student displays, and charts _____

B. Climate

Students on task _____
Time needed to change tasks _____
Students prepared for work _____
Student-to-teacher initiated contacts _____
Teacher voice _____

II. Diagnostic-Prescriptive Teaching
   A. Assessment and Appropriate Selection of Diagnostic Inventories

   B. Writing Behavioral Objectives

   C. Materials

Figure 17. Supervisory Report Form.

Fig. 17, *continued*

III. Strong Points Observed:

IV. Behavioral Objectives for Teacher:

V. Progress Toward Meeting Objectives:

    A. Satisfactory Progress
    B. Needs improvement in meeting objectives

VI. Teacher Reaction:

Date:

Additional Considerations:

Reports completed and returned promptly

Punctuality

Other

Signatures: _____ _____
            Teacher   Date   Supervisor   Date

103

Supervisory Report Form

Teacher Observed: _____   Time of Observation: ___:___ to ___:___

School and Class: _____   Date: _____

Number of Pupils: _____   Observer: _____

I. Classroom and School Variables
   A. Physical (as far as the teacher can control)

   Class Layout:

   External Noise, Heat, Light, Ventilation _adequate_
   Cleanliness, Orderliness _✓_
   Furniture appropriate and of right size _Yes_
   Materials, equipment, and resources (including supportive personnel)
      accessible and used _good_
   Safety precautions _adequate_
   Bulletin boards, student displays, and charts _good_

   B. Climate

   Students on task _adequate_
   Time needed to change tasks _good_
   Students prepared for work
   Student-to-teacher initiated contacts _often + appropriate_
   Teacher voice _good_

II. Diagnostic-Prescriptive Teaching
A. Assessment and Appropriate Selection of Diagnostic Inventories

Used both formal and informal reading assessments – seems to cover the ranges of achievement in the classroom

No assessment in math was observed.

B. Writing Behavioral Objectives

Adequate in reading, but nonexistent in math

C. Materials

Adequate

Figure 18. Completed Supervisory Report Form with hypothetical entries.

Fig. 18, *continued*

III. Strong Points Observed:

- Assessment of Reading
- Responses to academic behaviors
- Responded only to children seeking attention in a quiet way — hand raises or waiting turn

IV. Behavioral Objectives for Teacher:

Given consultation services of the District math consultant, Mr. Dobbs, Mrs. Brown will assess the children's math achievement and group children according to achievement within two months.

V. Progress Toward Meeting Objectives:

Previous objective of ignoring children who seek attention in disruptive ways seems to be completely mastered.

A. Satisfactory Progress ✓
B. Needs improvement in meeting objectives _____

VI. Teacher Reaction:

It's nice to see my efforts recognized.
I've meant to deal with the under and over achievers in Math for some time. Now I have the incentive and means to do so.

Date: _____

Additional Considerations:

Reports completed and returned promptly

Punctuality

Other

Signatures: _____ _____
            Teacher   Date

            _____ _____
            Supervisor   Date

107

The third item, "Materials," *(C)*, refers directly to the operational manner in which the teacher attempts to teach to the objective in question. The structure of the lesson and the criteria established for the objective are also considered. Perhaps most important is the system used by the teacher to record progress made toward meeting the objective. Do the materials lend themselves to recording the outcome of discrete trials, and does the teacher have materials and records for recording the outcome of those trials? Materials, then, is used in the broadest sense: materials for teaching, materials for recording the child's daily progress, and materials for recording long range progress.

Section III

Section III, "Strong Points Observed," forces the supervisor to be positive at a critical moment in that the next section will refer to areas where the teacher is in need of some improvement. In Section III, only very brief comments should be made of diagnostic-prescriptive techniques as these have already been covered in some detail. Ordinarily, sections of the teacher rapport form (Teacher Response to Student Behavior Form, Figures 4–7) in which the teacher has done well are referred to most often. The Teacher Response to Student Behavior Form is sufficiently complex so as to make it likely that any teacher will behave appropriately in some categories. In all but the most bizarre of circumstances, it will be easy for the supervisor to select positive qualities for comment. In the case of the excellent teacher for whom the comments might be too lengthy, a general statement with specific reference to most recent areas of improvement is recommended.

Usually there is a time lapse between observation and feedback, although delays of 24 hours or more should be avoided whenever possible. If the supervisor has some time before the teacher is free, Sections I, II, and III can be completed by the supervisor before the teacher arrives. The completion of the form will be thereby facilitated so that all items are completed before the teacher signs the form at the completion of the feedback session. *However, the supervisor should not complete the form beyond Section III without teacher input and teacher review of all information gathered by the supervisor.*

Section IV

In Section IV, an objective is to be established for the teacher. The teacher will then know exactly what teacher behaviors need to be changed in effort to continue to approximate the ideal. Generally, it is best to limit the number of objectives for the teacher to one or two per observation in order to avoid overwhelming the teacher. In the case where a great deal of improvement is needed, it is better to increase the number of observations rather than the number of objectives established per observation. At the other extreme, there may be no objective of much importance apparent for the excellent teacher. When an objective cannot be identified (very rare) or is of relatively minor importance, fewer observations are needed.

The supervisor should not establish the objective for the teacher without input from the teacher. Ideally, the teacher establishes an objective with which the supervisor agrees. Upon review of rapport observations as well as all other observations recorded in Sections I, II, and III, most teachers will be able to identify an objective for themselves or at least an area of concern that the supervisor may help them mold into an objective. The objective will be better understood and accepted in cases where the objective is mutually established. In the case of the uncooperative teacher, fortunately also rare, the supervisor in accord with the supervisor's role may impose an objective. Whatever the case may be, the objective should be worded in such a way that progress toward the objective can be objectively measured in future observations. An objective that does not lend itself to assessment is badly worded and best avoided altogether. Examples of possible objectives for teachers follow:

> Given 2 months, Mr. Brown will have selected and administered a diagnostic reading test appropriate to the reading series used in the district to each child in his class.

Given 1 month and weekly observational feedback, Mrs. Smith will increase the frequency with which she gives attention to appropriate social behavior to a point where it exceeds the frequency with which she gives attention to inappropriate social behavior.

Given 6 weeks, Mr. Jones will have established and recorded individualized behavioral objectives in self-help for each of the three children in need of dressing and grooming skills.

Given weekly feedback, Miss Doe will increase the ratio of novel or enthusiastic positive responses to correct academic behavior from a ratio of 1 enthusiastic to 10 knowledge-of-results responses (1:10) to a ratio of 1 enthusiastic to 2 knowledge-of-results responses (1:2).

Section V

In Section V, a record is made regarding progress toward meeting previously established objectives. If objectives are well worded with clear criteria based on data gathered during the observation, completion of Section V should be relatively simple. In the event that several objectives have been identified, developing new objectives may best be temporarily avoided. Repeated failure to approximate reasonable objectives over a lengthy period of time suggests that the teacher either:

1. Does not understand the objectives
2. Is unable to moniter his/her own behavior
3. Refuses to cooperate

The number of observations made needs to be increased in order to provide as much feedback and opportunity to improve as possible. Should the problem or problems continue even with the supervisory support provided, the teacher may be unable to improve past or present levels of functioning within the support limits of the system. The evaluative outcome is apparent and the system may elect whatever changes seem most desirable.

Section VI

In Section VI, the teacher is given the opportunity to make any comment that he or she desires. The teacher should be encouraged to offer at least a note regarding the teacher's feelings about the objective.

FREQUENCY OF COMPLETE AND FORMAL OBSERVATION

The complete and formal observation, as described, is certainly time consuming. The experienced supervisor can anticipate at least 45 minutes of observation and recording, 15 minutes of completing items on forms, and 15 to 30 minutes of feedback and discussion with the teacher. Very few systems have the supervisory manpower to make such complex observations at high frequencies such as once per week. More likely, the supervisor will be able to make three or perhaps four complete observations per school year per teacher. If these were the only observations made, feedback would be too infrequent to promote change, especially in rapport skills. Less time-consuming observations must also be made for the system to reach its pragmatic potential.

FEEDBACK AND TRAINING

Once the formal observation is made, one or two points of major concern will be isolated in the teacher's objectives. Observation and feedback in regard to the selected concerns may take only a few minutes. Records of assessment and objectives can be checked in very little time and suggestions given in a minute or two more. Extensive training, as in the case of the teacher who does not know how to compose a satisfactory objective, can often be done on a small group in-service basis between the supervisor and the supervisees in need of training. When objectives relate to rapport skills or the Teacher Response to Student Behavior Form, the supervisor may stop by for 10 or 15 minutes, use the form, and leave it with the teacher with a brief verbal comment about how the information recorded relates to the teacher's objective. In effect, the complete observation isolates the supervisor's attention on the more frequent and briefer observations until enough time passes to merit another complete observation. As a result, the system becomes viable in regard to supervisor's time within the supervisor/supervisee ratios established by most school systems or states. The Supervisory Report Form (Figure 18, pages 104–107), completed with hypothetical information, serves as an example.

Chapter 6
Summary

Ever since teachers have been formally supervised, much of teacher supervision has been notoriously vague and ineffective. Teaching has been accepted as an art in which characteristics associated with quality change from individual to individual. Inasmuch as direct supervision has neither been operationalized nor recognized as important, supervisors have been given lower or middle management responsibilities to the near exclusion of supervision itself. Yet the need to be observed and to get feedback is recognized as important to any task with high performance standards. Observing students and providing feedback is the primary role of most teachers. Surely then, the teacher needs feedback as well.

Today, thanks to research in learning theory and educational technology, the qualities of "good teaching" can be better defined than ever before. As the qualities can be operationalized, so too are the characteristics of the "good teacher." There still remains an undefinable, or yet to be defined, "artlike" quality of good teaching, but to a lesser degree. The teacher should be a positive feedback agent who is also consistent and appropriate. The teacher should also begin teaching from what the student already knows. Therefore, there must be some sort of assessment of the students' present level of functioning. Instructional plans should be formulated to begin at points approximating the assessed achievement level. Exactly how the teacher accomplishes these tasks will vary from personality to personality and curriculum to curriculum. Different teachers may select different words for praising success or for correcting error. A different reading series will suggest a different assessment format and different lessons. Yet the differences are minor. The process of good teaching is the same.

The preceding chapters explain a system for observing and recording the process of good teaching. The system can be adapted to a special education class for multiply handicapped preschoolers or an advanced trigonometry section in a senior high school. Its strength and novelty lie in the identification of various parts of the process and the operationalization of each of the parts into an observable set of behaviors. The parts include teacher rapport, assessment, and lesson planning. Forms are provided, described, and explained that allow for systematic observation and evaluation of each of the parts. Strengths and weaknesses in each are identifiable. Therefore, the teacher can also be assessed. Based on the assessment, objectives can be established for the teacher. It is the supervisor's task to facilitate progress toward an objective just as the teacher does for students. The teacher can systematically approximate an ideal. The quality of teaching can be improved and maintained through supervision.

Perhaps of equal importance is the operationalization of the supervisory observation into a system with a discrete beginning and end. Administrators who place a priority on improving the quality of teaching, a higher priority than any other task that can be assigned to supervisors, can maintain that priority through supervision. Given a discrete supervisory system, the administrator can require some frequency of observation that must be minimally met before any other task assigned to the supervisory role. The school system in which real supervision is done only when all other responsibilities are met should become a thing of the past.

Finally, the ideal effect, although the probability of any ideal is remote, should be conceptualized. This system provides the necessary data to evaluate and potentially to improve performance of teachers in three discrete but related areas: rapport, assessment, and curriculum programming. Given either teacher personalities that are receptive to and able to change and/or relaxed tenure clauses, it should be possible for a school system to develop a teaching staff that is uniformly exceptional in all three respects. If all teachers in the system were positive, appropriate, and consistent managers, students would, for reasons of respondent conditioning, enjoy school and like both teachers and the curriculum. Coercion, common in today's schools, would be rare and perhaps never necessary. The teachers' administrators should follow the same management principles so that teachers too would enjoy their roles more than is usually the case. Since students are the managers of the future, the effect ripples to influence society as a whole.

With all teachers skilled at assessment, the ideal school system would have extensive assessment resources, materials, and guidelines. Teachers would know what each student had achieved to whatever extent necessary. Instruction could, either on an individual or group basis, be directed as accurately as possible toward the needs of each student.

The long and short term goals for each student could be operationalized and made known to all interested parties, including the student and parents. Records could reflect the rate of goal attainment so that inadequate procedures could be discarded, adequate procedures recognized, and instruction in general could become self-improving (Piper, 1977). Ambiguity regarding student evaluation or promotion could be completely eliminated. All of the advantages of establishing objectives, cited earlier, could be achieved and the side effects of each advantage recognized. Students who learn basic tool skills ahead of schedule could be released from the highly structured programming to pursue topics of academic interest. Considerations now reserved for the conspicuously gifted child could become commonplace.

Although the ideal may be unrealistic, the system provides for its attainment. Educators and educational administrators of all sorts may establish their long range objectives accordingly.

References

Amidon, E. J., and Flanders, N. A. 1971. *The Role of the Teacher in the Classroom.* Association for Productive Teaching, St. Paul.

Axelrod, S. 1977. *Behavior Modification for the Classroom Teacher.* McGraw-Hill Book Company, New York.

Barr, A. S. 1931. *An Introduction to the Scientific Study of Classroom Supervision.* D. Appleton-Century Co., New York.

Becker, W. C., Madsen, C. H., Arnold, C. R., and Thomas, D. R. 1967. The contingent use of teacher attention and praise in reducing classroom behavior problems. *Journal of Special Education, 1,* 287–307.

Bennie, W. A. 1972. *Supervising Clinical Experiences in the Classroom.* Harper & Row Publishers, New York.

Brown, L., and York, R. 1974. Developing Programs for Severely Handicapped Students: Teacher Training and Classroom Instruction. In Brown, Williams, & Crowner (eds.), *A Collection of Papers and Programs Related to Public School Services for Severely Handicapped Students.* Madison Public Schools, Madison, Wisconsin, pp. 1–18.

Buchanen, C. D. 1968. *Programmed Reading, Sullivan As-*

sociates Program, Revised Edition. McGraw-Hill, New York.

Durrell, D. D. 1973. *Beginning Language Concepts.* Borg-Warner Systems 80, Arlington Heights, Il.

Flanders, N. A. 1970. *Analyzing Teacher Behavior.* Addison-Wesley, Reading, Mass.

Hall, R. V., Panyon, M., Rabon, D., and Broden, M. 1968. Instructing beginning teachers in reinforcement procedures which improve classroom control. *Journal of Applied Behavior Analysis, 1,* 315–322.

Hamp, E., O'Donnell, M., and Greenlaw, J. 1974. *Patterns in Design for Reading.* Harper & Row, East Brunswick, N.J.

Haring, N. G. 1977. Measurement and Evaluation Procedures for Programming with the Severely and Profoundly Handicapped. In E. Sontag (ed.), *Educational Programming for the Severely and Profoundly Handicapped.* Council for Exceptional Children.

Harris, L. A., and Smith, C. B. 1972. *Reading Instruction Through Diagnostic Teaching.* Holt, Rinehart, & Winston, Inc., New York.

Horton, G. O. 1975. Generalization of teacher behavior as a function of subject matter specific discrimination training. *Journal of Applied Behavior Analysis, 8,* 311–319.

Lucio, W. H., and McNeil, J. D. 1962. *Supervision: A Synthesis of Thought and Action.* McGraw-Hill Book Company, Inc., New York.

Mager, R. F. 1962. *Preparing Instructional Objectives.* Fearon Publishers, Belmont, Cal.

Mann, P. H., and Suiter, P. 1974. *Handbook in Diagnostic Teaching: A Learning Disabilities Approach.* Allyn and Bacon, Boston.

Marks, J. R., Stoops, E., and King-Stoops, J. 1978. *Handbook of Educational Supervision: A guide for the Practitioner.* Allyn and Bacon, Boston.

O'Leary, K. D., and O'Leary, S. G. 1972. *Classroom Manage-*

ment: The Successful Use of Behavior Modification. Pergamon Press, Inc., New York.

Peter, L. J. 1972. *Individual Instruction: Prescriptive Teaching System.* McGraw-Hill Book Company, New York.

Piper, T. 1977. A synergistic view of behavioral objectives and behavior modification. *Educational Technology, 17,* 26–30.

Public Law 94-142. Education for All Handicapped Children Act of 1975 (November 29, 1975).

Ringer, V. M. J. 1973. The use of a "token helper" in the management of classroom behavior problems and in teaching training. *Journal of Applied Behavior Analysis, 6,* 671–677.

Simon, A., and Boyer, E. G. 1974. *Mirrors for Behavior: An Anthology of Observation Instruments.* Research for Better Schools, Inc., Philadelphia.

Tucker, D. J., and Horner, R. D. 1977. Competency-based Training of Paraprofessional Teaching Associates in Education of the Severely and Profoundly Handicapped. In E. Sontag (ed.), *Educational Programming for the Severely and Profoundly Handicapped.* Council for Exceptional Children.

Index

11